EGYPT UNDER MUBARAK

EGYPT
UNDER
MUBARAK

EDITED BY CHARLES TRIPP AND ROGER OWEN

Centre for Near and Middle Eastern Studies,
School of Oriental and African Studies

ROUTLEDGE
London and New York

First published 1989
by Routledge
11 New Fetter Lane, London EC4P 4EE
29 West 35th Street, New York, NY 10001

Printed in Great Britain by
Billing & Sons Ltd, Worcester

British Library Cataloguing in Publication Data

Egypt under Mubarak
  1. Egypt. Social conditions
  I. Tripp, Charles II. Owen, Roger
  962'.055
  ISBN 0-415-03887-1

Library of Congress Cataloging in Publication Data

Egypt under Mubarak / edited by Charles Tripp and Roger Owen.
      p. cm. — (A SOAS Middle East Centre study)
  "Papers . . . written for a conference held at the School of
Oriental and African Studies in May 1987" — Pref.
  Includes index.
  ISBN 0-415-03887-1
    1. Egypt – Politics and government – 1981-   – Congresses. 2. Egypt –
Economic conditions – 1952- – Congresses. I. Tripp, Charles.
II. Owen, Edward Roger John. III. Series.
DT107.87.E37 1989
962'.05–dc19   88-32177

Table of Contents

v

Preface

It is the intention of the essays in this book to examine some of the causes and consequences of the numerous crises within the Egyptian political and economic systems. The essay by Ayubi examines the strategies deployed by and the resources available to those who rule the state in their attempts to deal with diverse social pressures to the advantage of their own power. Makram-Ebeid studies the question from the point of view of the organised opposition, as it treads a cautious path between newly found civil liberties and the authoritarian habits of the government. Shukrullah presents a view of the structural crises and underlying processes of the Egyptian state, examining in particular the way these have affected the forms of political struggle during the past decade or so. Amin offers a link between the political, sociological and economic explanations of Egypt's current crisis by arguing that many of its manifestations are due to the very rapid rate of social mobility which has characterised Egyptian society since the revolution of 1952. Butter examines the scale of Egypt's external debt and the resources, both financial and political, available to the government in its efforts to devise a long-term strategy of economic renewal. In the agricultural sector, Commander looks critically at the policies pursued by the Egyptian government, particularly the strategies of mechanisation, in its attempt to increase productivity in this vital sector. In conclusion, Tripp examines the ways in which the moral and structural constraints upon the activities of the Egyptian government affect the ways in which it conducts its relations with the states in its immediate vicinity.

These essays discuss both the legacy with which President Mubarak must come to terms as head of the Egyptian state, as well as the strategies he and his colleagues have devised in order to cope with that legacy. The structures and processes which characterise these efforts are, therefore, both cause and effect of factors beyond the immediate control of the President himself, rooted as they are either in the modern history of Egyptian political development or in the economic and military concerns of the world beyond Egypt's borders. The crucial question is whether the Egyptian political order can survive the crises generated by these processes, given the limited resources at the disposal of those who would maintain that order. These limitations are not simply material, of course, but may also apply to the conceptual underpinnings of the policies devised to meet the challenge of crisis. In this respect, it is worth asking whether the present administration in Egypt has the capacity to go beyond the *idées reçues* of an authoritarian political tradition and to perceive that the crisis is not simply one of the political order, narrowly viewed, but rather of the political community of Egypt itself.

As such, it would seem to demand a more thoroughgoing reassessment of the relationship of the individual to the state than has hitherto been officially sanctioned, let alone promoted. A development of this nature is clearly fundamental to the long-term future of political order in Egypt. However, the danger is that the severity of the problems confronting those who might be expected to initiate such a policy will elevate short-term crisis management to the level of high strategy. This, in turn, runs the risk of eroding the very resources on which they must depend in order to face the crises to come. It is hoped that the essays in this book will give the reader some sense of the nature of those resources, the capacity of the government to manage their deployment and the consequences of such management for the future of the Egyptian state.

Acknowledgements

The effort and hard work involved in the production of a book of this kind incur many debts of gratitude. The editors would like, therefore, to thank all those whose assistance made possible the conference in which this book originated. They acknowledge with thanks the financial and institutional support of the School of Oriental and African Studies, as well as the financial assistance of the British Academy. The conference could not have taken place without the participation of the Centre of Near and Middle Eastern Studies at SOAS, whose staff were responsible for the efficient organisation of the meeting. Amongst those deserving of particular mention in this regard are the Director of the Centre, Dr Tony Allan, and his assistants, Richard Brow and Bridget Harney. However, a special debt of thanks is due to Diana Crosby. Her patience and skill in mastering the many functions of copy-editor have greatly facilitated the production of the book itself, and the editors and authors wish to acknowledge with gratitude the tireless enthusiasm which she brought to the task.

Charles Tripp and Roger Owen
London and Oxford, March 1988

1

GOVERNMENT AND THE STATE IN EGYPT TODAY

Nazih N. Ayubi

President Husni Mubarak has inherited a complex legacy from the Nasser and Sadat eras. This can represent a 'mixed blessing'; on the one hand it puts at his disposal an array of laws, institutions and practices that tend to work in favour of the head of the Egyptian state. On the other hand, it burdens him with responsibility for the outcome of state policies initiated before his term (i.e. the emergence of the so-called 'infitah mafia', or the bitter harvest of the peace treaty with Israel). If he does not change them, they count as his own. The purpose of this chapter is to survey the main features of the governmental structure and the representative machinery that were largely inherited by Mubarak, and to illustrate the way in which the Mubarak regime has made use of these institutions since he came to power at the end of 1981.

The governmental structure

The Egyptian system of government is in a period of transition, which, among other things, is characterised by a number of contradictions. While in principle a policy of economic and political liberalisation is being promoted, the Presidency remains dominant - even in economic matters. The size of the public 'Establishment' continues - especially in terms of employment - to grow (at a time when the role of the public sector is declining) and

1

the bureaucracy shows no signs of ceasing to be restrictive and constraining. Furthermore, the 'control' functions of the government remain more immediately felt than are its advocated developmental and welfare functions. Or, as some may put it, there is too much government where it is least needed, and too little government where it is needed most (cf. Ayubi, 1982b).

The Presidency

Egypt is a presidential state. Owing to political culture and legal traditions, the President is the dominant political and governmental authority in Egypt. Any important policy or project must normally have the 'blessing' of the President before it can proceed with a reasonable prospect of success. Presidential powers include the right to propose, veto and promulgate legislation. When the People's Assembly is not in session, the President may issue decrees that have the force of law (and which are ratified later by the Assembly), while under some circumstances, and by investiture of the Assembly, he may, and does, issue decree laws whether or not the Assembly is in session (ARE, 1971: Articles 108, 112, and 147). Under Sadat the Presidency was given such a delegation for issuing laws by decree in all economic matters, in addition to an earlier delegation for the purchase of arms. Following the 'food riots' of January 1977, President Sadat declared a number of emergency decrees and called for a referendum to endorse them; this subsequently became a recurring practice.

Linked to the Presidency is the Central Agency for Public Mobilisation and Statistics (CAPMAS), headed for many years after its inception in 1964 by an ex-army general. CAPMAS is the main 'data bank' in Egypt, and is important both as a source of vital information for any project, and also for its controlling role (since any sizeable statistical study conducted in Egypt has to secure the approval of the Agency in advance). It is high in the governmental hierarchy, and should, in principle, report directly to the President. Affiliated also to the Presidency is the Central Auditing Agency

(CAA), which is the supreme control and evaluation agency for the public sector and for the economic activities of the state.

Then there is the unique office of the 'Socialist Public Prosecutor', which was incorporated for the first time in the 1971 Constitution, that is, after Sadat came to power and when the regime's policies were being re-oriented away from socialism. The Prosecutor is appointed by the President and is subject to the control of the People's Assembly. His jurisdiction is ambiguous. He seems to have a mixture of legal, administrative and also political 'control' functions, and can be likened to a parliamentary ombudsman, state prosecutor, and political commissar, all put together, while his duties include 'securing the safety of the society and its political system and the preservation of the socialist achievements and commitment to socialist behaviour' (ARE, 1977: 131-132).

Other institutions directly associated with the president are the prestigious, but basically advisory, National Specialised Councils, introduced in 1974, whose declared purpose is to assist the President in drawing up national plans and policies by surveying the available resources and their potential, and advising on the optimum utilisation of existing capabilities, towards the fulfilment of the objectives of the state.

Of course, presidents who assume various posts and enjoy extensive powers are by no means an exception in the developing countries. The paradox here is the fact that Sadat had made the advocacy of 'freedom' and 'democracy' the main point when contrasting his regime with that of President Nasser, yet he ended up with more posts and titles to his name than Nasser ever did. In addition to his favourite title of 'Elder of the Egyptian Family', Sadat in 1981 had the following official posts: President of the Republic, Prime Minister, Supreme Commander of the Armed Forces, Higher Chief of the Police Forces, Higher Chief of the Judiciary, Head of the National Democratic Party (the ruling party), and Commissioner on all military and economic matters and accords touching on national security.

Sadat also added to his power by making the number of presidential periods indefinite, and he made frequent use of popular referenda in preference to 'normal' legislative procedures. He enacted a law for the 'protection of morals from shame' ('*aib;* signifying taboo, extremely shameful and 'not done'), and 'Morals' Courts were formed to deal with cases that were not covered by ordinary laws. Sweeping powers were given to the leadership in dealing with cases that could be classified as harming 'national integration', 'social peace', or 'religious and community values'. By the end of Sadat's era, Egypt had truly become a boss-state (*état-rais*) (Mirel, 1982: 242ff).

The Cabinet

The President determines the general policies of the state, and the Cabinet, headed by the Premier, supervises their implementation. To fulfil its functions, the Cabinet may issue 'decisions' pertaining to economic or other matters. 'Decisions' may also be issued, in descending order, by the Prime Minister, and by individual ministers and governors. Most ministries have a number of public companies and sometimes public authorities and public organizations belonging to them. On the other hand, all ministries dealing with matters of production, finance, trade and public sector, are usually clustered together in an interministerial committee, often known as the 'Economic Group'. Another interministerial group that is particularly active in the 1980s is the so-called 'Policies Committee'.

The Cabinet tends to be composed, as it came to be under Nasser, mainly of 'technocrats', with academic or professional backgrounds, especially engineers, economists, and university professors. Of the 163 ministers who took portfolios under Sadat (1971-1981), 131 were of a civilian career background and of the following professional specialisations: university professors 52; engineers 34; lawyers 12; diplomats 6; economists 4; *ulama* 5; others 18. In addition there were 32 ministers of a military career background, of whom 18 were professional officers; 9 were military-technocrats, and 5 intelligence men. The main difference which distinguished the composition of cabinets in the Sadat era from that of Nasser's era, and which also characterises the Mubarak era, is the decline in the recruitment of ministers of a military career background from 33.6 per cent of all (131) ministers recruited in the Nasserist period, to 20 per cent of all (163) ministers recruited in the Sadat era (Badruddin, in Hilal *et al.* 1982: 90-96). Of all (50) ministers who served in the first three cabinets under Mubarak 10 per cent were of a military career background (CPSS,1986: 325).

In many ways CAPMAS enjoys the role one would expect a central planning agency to enjoy in a country like Egypt. By contrast, the formal planning function is entrusted to an ordinary ministry, not in any way higher in legal or in functional status than any other ministry. This is a continuation from the Nasserist era. Historically the Ministry of Planning was never very influential, as it really emerged after the preparation of the first, and to all intents and purposes, the last, Five Year Development Plan (1959/60 to 1960/65). The 1967 defeat and its economic and political aftermath had changed the circumstances, and what has actually happened since then is the preparation of annual public investment programmes. It was basically the Annual State Budget which functioned as the major tool of direction in the economic system, while the Central Auditing Agency continued to play a major role in the financial control of the public sector.

The growing number of joint ventures and other private enterprises since the adoption of infitah in 1974 has also made the grip of the planning machinery over the economy as a whole, very weak indeed. The abolition of the central 'Pricing Agency', the gradual removal (partly under International Monetary Fund recommendations) of various 'consumer' and 'production' subsidies, and the phasing out of many protective customs, means that the real grip of the planning machinery over the national economy is weakening. Indeed, the government has become so dependent on external sources for financing investment that the 'department of international co-operation' has been affiliated to the Ministry of Planning in recent years.

The Bureaucracy

The Egyptian bureaucracy remains large, and continues to expand in terms of units, personnel, salaries, and expenditure. The disproportionate growth of the public 'Establishment' is not a new phenomenon in Egypt. With the 1952 Revolution, however, the public bureaucracy grew more rapidly and extensively, under the impact of the regime's policies for expanding industrial activities, welfare services and free education. This growth was particularly striking after the 'socialist measures' of the early 1960s, which involved wide nationalisations of industry, trade and finance, worker participation in management and profits, and also an extensive programme for social services and insurance.

The public bureaucracy grew steadily in size between 1952 and 1970, when measured by the number of administrative units, the size of employment, the development of wages and salaries and of current expenditure. The most notable changes can be summarised thus: from 1962/63 to 1969/70, the national income of Egypt increased by 68 per cent, resting on an increase in the labour force of no more than 20 per cent. Yet at the same time, posts in the public bureaucracy had increased by 70 per cent and salaries by 123 per cent. Thus, the rate of bureaucratic growth had quite exceeded the rate of growth in population, employment and production.

The impetus of institutional growth continued, however, under its own momentum, even though the role of the government and the scope of the public sector started to diminish in importance. For example, the 1975 budget indicated that current expenditures and costs had risen to the tune of LE4747.6 million, of which LE652.8 million went to wages and salaries. Current expenditure accounted for 66.2 per cent of the total financial outlay of the budget, whereas wages and salaries accounted for 10.5 per cent of that total. This

6

trend continued in the following years so that in 1979, for instance, the state budget involved total current expenditure and outlays of LE9172.9 million, of which LE1257 million were for wages and salaries. This was also accompanied by a serious rise in the budgetary deficits.

The public bureaucracy (that is, the civil service and the public sector excluding enterprise workers) employed in 1978 over 1.9 million people. If state companies are added, the public 'Establishment' was employing at the beginning of 1978 about 3.2 million officials and workers. Further, the public bureaucracy continues to receive the bulk of the country's university and college graduates, and appoints annually around 100,000 new graduates (cf. Ayubi, 1982b). By the mid-1980s, it was estimated that well over three million individuals were employed in the central and local government as well as in the public sector (excluding public companies). Furthermore, the share of wages and salaries to total current expenditures had risen from 19 per cent in 1974/5 to 29 per cent in 1984/5 (CPSS, 1986:351).

The representative machinery

Part of the liberalisation policy in the 1970s involved extending the scope for political activity, and this gave a potentially different significance to the possible role of the legislature and political parties in directing and supervising public activity (cf. Hinnebusch, 1985). The legislature consists basically of a uni-cameral assembly (the People's Assembly) which has an elected membership (currently for 448 seats), in addition to up to ten members appointed by the President. Half the members of the Assembly should be 'workers and peasants', a provision which also applies to other local and popular councils, and which represents one of the few political legacies retained from the Nasserist era.

Nobody, however, could guarantee such representation for the workers and peasants in political parties, as the country was moving

7

away from the formula of 'alliance of the working forces of the people', that had been adopted under Nasser, towards a more 'pluralistic' system. In the early 1970s, a drive towards 'democracy', in the sense of liberalisation and multi-partyism, acquired some momentum, following the 'corrective movement'(*harakat al-tashi*) of 15 May 1971, and the promulgation of the Egyptian Permanent Constitution in the same year. A certain formula for semi-pluralism within, and then outside, the Arab Socialist Union (ASU), was eventually approved, the process starting in 1974 with a review of the ASU's structure and function. Plurality of political 'orientations' within the single organisation was accepted in 1975. Platforms (*manabir)*, were then to be permitted within the organisation to represent certain ideological and political trends. A thirst for political activity was revealed by the application for nearly forty platforms, and after much debating of the matter, it was authoritatively decided that only three organs within the ASU would be allowed, representing the 'right', the 'centre' and the 'left'. One condition for allowing these organisations was that they should accept a number of guiding principles: 'democratic socialism', 'social peace', and 'national unity'.

The three new organisations were allowed to adopt programmes and to produce lists for the People's Assembly elections in 1976. This resulted in an overwhelming victory for the regime's 'centre' organisation, as the centre (government) 'Misr Arab Socialist' organisation received 82 per cent of the seats (Mar'i, 1977: 32). It is undeniable, however, that these elections were conducted under the umbrella of the 'government party', which had more access to financial, logistic and communicational facilities than had other organisations.

In November 1976, these three organisations were allowed to transform themselves into legalised political parties. Nevertheless, it should be observed that the regime applied its authority in deciding which political parties would be allowed and the reasons why. It may have made some sense to deny religious groups the right to form a political party on the grounds that their ideals, which are religiously oriented, would be bound to act against 'national unity'. Yet it does not make much sense, for example, to have refused to allow a Nasserist party to form on the grounds that those who considered themselves 'true Nasserists' *should* join the centre party. After hesitation and delay, the pre-revolutionary *Wafd* party was also allowed officially to reform early in 1978. However, after a few months, this party was to dissolve itself because of what its leaders considered to be government persecution of their party's policies and activities (though it re-emerged later, under Mubarak).

The 1979 parliamentary elections gave the government party even more dominance over the People's Assembly than it had had after the previous elections. Under its new name of the Nationalist Democratic Party, it acquired at least 92 per cent of the seats in the Assembly, in addition to most of the thirty newly allocated seats in important constituencies for women candidates (cf. Hilal *et al.*, 1982). The Assembly, however, was abruptly dismissed, following a referendum in April 1979 about 'peace and democracy' which was meant to ratify Egypt's treaty with Israel. In May 1980 another referendum amended the constitution and ratified the establishment of a Consultative Assembly (*majlis al-shura*) that was to be formed partly by election (140 members), and partly by appointment (70 members). As such, this *majlis* would be even more easily controlled than the fairly docile People's Assembly. The role of this new *majlis* is to act in an advisory capacity to the President and to the People's Assembly (ARE, 1984: 12-13).

The People's Assembly has attempted to consolidate its power and prestige in the political system, and an important example and 'test case' for this in the mid - to late 1970s was the heated controversy that was aroused over the Pyramids Plateau project. Land on the Pyramids Plateau was leased to a foreign firm for ninety-nine years without approval of the Assembly. Subsequently the project - which involved development of the land for tourist and recreational purposes - was fiercely criticised on cultural grounds, and the group opposing the project began to gain considerable professional and popular support, eventually turning into a serious pressure group, that obliged the original agreement to be cancelled entirely.

In general, one could say that the borders between the jurisdiction and the scope of activity of the various political institutions - especially the representative and legislative ones - are still undergoing a process of formation, and that many political and economic actions are still based more on 'bargaining' than on clear legal principles. In this act of bargaining there can be little doubt that it is the executive branch of government, and particularly the President, that normally has the upper hand.

The Mubarak regime

President Mubarak has inherited a complex legacy from the Nasser and Sadat eras, and with it a *mélange* of policies and institutions that date back to the period of 'socialist transformation', or else to the days of the 'open door policy'.

The social base of the State that Mubarak inherited cannot be separated from the realignment of classes that took place under infitah, and which brought to the fore an alliance between elements from the pre-revolutionary semi-aristocracy, the state bourgeoisie of the 1960s, and the commercial/financial cliques of the infitah era (cf. Ayubi, 1982a; Imam, 1986). Yet it should be clear that the role of the state bourgeoisie has not really been seriously reduced, since the State continues to allocate to itself a significant proportion of national resources. In particular, a large expansion in the control and repressive organs of the state has been taking place since the 1970s as already indicated, e.g. the central security forces, State Security Courts and 'Morals' Courts, the Public Prosecutor's functions, as well as the bureaucracy, the armed forces, and the State information machine in general. Furthermore, much of the country's growth in bureaucratic expenditure in recent years has been directed to the country's higher political and administrative echelons (cf. Ayubi, 1982b; Ghunaim, 1986).

10

A further number of contradictions also characterise the current position of the Egyptian State in society:

1. Although the State machine is more amenable to the interests of the newly-emerged class conglomeration of infitah, it does strive to play the role of the arbiter between the various 'fractions' of the evolving bourgeoisie, and even to maintain a certain degree of 'relative autonomy' vis-à-vis the conflicting class interests in the society. Because of this, the State appears from time to time to reach a point of confrontation with the financial/commercial bourgeoisie in particular, whenever attempts are made to rationalise importation practices, free zone activities, pricing policies, etc. This confrontation reached one of its peaks in early 1985 when the State tried to regulate the movement of money and credit within the economy.

2. The desire by the State to maintain its political and economic hold has led, at a time of growing private capital, to the State offering various privileges to the higher echelons of the bureaucracy in an attempt to persuade them to support the State's efforts to safeguard the general movement of capital. Furthermore, members of these higher bureaucratic echelons are usually the ones who earn further income through the symbiotic linkages that they often manage to build up with the private, domestic, Arab and foreign sectors. Income differentials have widened between the top of the bureaucracy and its lower levels of State officials and public sector workers and technicians, etc. This probably explains the rebellion by some lower levels and 'peripheral' sections of the State over its core in recent years, which was manifested in repeated strikes and sit-ins by public sector workers, and which reached a dangerous level with the mutiny of the Central Security forces against State authority early in 1986.

3. The Islamic trend, which was initially encouraged by the Sadat regime, has found its main appeal among the young educated groups who have been hurt by the outcomes of infitah. Such groups have now rebelled against this very State and have begun to attack both its symbols and its institutions.

11

4. Although certainly interested in political stability in Egypt, some of the external allies of the Egyptian State at the present time seem to be in some ways interested in weakening the State machine and shaking its economic hegemony in the society. This manifests itself in the policies of several foreign and international 'aid' donors (The United States Agency for International Development, The International Monetary Fund, and before them, The Gulf Organisation for the Development of Egypt) which strive to strengthen the private sector and to consolidate economic and political decentralisation.

As the country approached the mid-1980s, some characteristics of the Mubarak regime became increasingly clear. Of these, the following are of particular importance:

1. Consolidation of the Mubarak regime was in power under a political formula that was only partly different from that of the Sadat era, the main difference being one of 'style' rather than basic substance.

2. Continuation of the deficits in the balance of payments and in the state budget, combined with a growing 'rentier' orientation for the economy as a whole. These realities had immediate social repercussions.

3. Continuation of a basically Western-oriented foreign policy while improving relations with the Soviet Union and reviving ties with the non-aligned countries.

4. A small but definite degree of improvement in Egypt's relations with most other Arab countries.

After a few flirtations with certain aspects of Nasserism, and after a short-lived campaign against corruption, the regime appeared to continue with basically the same personnel as from the Sadat era. A minor degree of discipline was imposed on the policy of infitah , although its main thrust remained unchanged. A degree of *rapprochement* began to be achieved with other Arab countries, without sacrificing the 1979 Egyptian-Israeli peace treaty, and a measure of political liberalisation was introduced with some (but not all) political parties being allowed to function, but with the tight grip of the government and security apparatus making it clear as to who would continue to rule.

In terms of leadership style, Mubarak's rule, has been based on a low key, businesslike style, that, in addition to its reputation for honesty and clean-handedness, was quite careful and reserved in its approach to issues and problems. This was a style that seemed unlikely to generate strong emotions among the populace, and which appeared well suited to a society that had reached something of a crossroads as far as its future direction was concerned, following an era of two leaders whose policies were different but whose 'presence' was closely felt everywhere.

According to some observers, the real Mubarak era started only in 1984. The first parliamentary elections held under the new regime took place in May of that year, according to a rather curious new electoral law, based on proportional representation (cf. Sayid-Ahmad, 1984). According to this law, no parties were allowed representation in Parliament unless they obtained at least eight per cent of all national votes (i.e. some 423,000 votes in the 1984 elections). All votes (and seats) acquired by those political parties that did not reach the required percentage, were added automatically to those of the winning party, which also monopolised the thirty seats allocated exclusively for women in the People's Assembly (this provision for women's representation was cancelled in the 1987 elections). The ruling National Democratic Party achieved 72.9 per cent of the votes and 87 per cent of the seats in the People's Assembly (total number of seats 448), the right wing Wafd party 15 per cent of the votes and 13 per cent of the seats, the Socialist Labour Party 7.73 per cent of the vote and no seats, the left wing Progressive Rally *Tajammu'* Party 4.1 per cent of the votes and no seats, and the Liberals' Party 0.65 per cent of the votes and no seats. The elections made it clear, therefore, that the ruling party, headed by Mubarak himself, was well in control. But the extent to which this 'control' was actually responsible for the results of the elections remained controversial for quite some time.

One obvious thing was that the ruling party fared much better in the countryside, where the government's grip over local government and the security machine is tighter. The opposition, by contrast, registered impressive victories in the large cities, gaining 38.4 per cent of all votes in Cairo, 32.7 per cent in Alexandria, 36 per cent in Suez, and as much as 53.3 per cent of all votes in Port Said.

There has always been a question as to whether (and when) President Mubarak will launch his own 'revolution within the Revolution', as did Nasser, and Sadat before him. Nasser had established himself firmly in power in 1954, two years after the eruption of the July 1952 Revolution, and started his main economic transformations in 1956 with the nationalisation of the Suez Canal company and other foreign concerns. After replacing Nasser in 1970, Sadat declared his 'corrective revolution' in 1971, and formalised his 'open door' policy in 1974. Mubarak made a point of saying that he was neither a Nasser nor a Sadat, but whether he intended to be something in between these two, or something all his own, has remained somewhat of an open question. It could safely be said that with the 1984 elections Mubarak had established himself well in power, yet he has not found it necessary or possible to rid the regime of several of the 'Sadat factions'.

In principle, the President enjoys tremendous powers, especially under the existing 'emergency laws' that were passed after the assassination of Sadat in 1981, yet Mubarak has chosen not to use them, either to change the composition of the ruling elite, or to make important shifts in the socio-economic system along the lines of Nasser's 'socialist transformations' or Sadat's policy of infitah. He continues to muddle through, pursuing basically the same policies (infitah and 'peace') and relying on the same political party. Although political liberalisation has progressed noticeably, the 'Sadatists' alliance is most intent on preventing real competition.

The 1987 elections

The Parties Law

Although political liberalisation has advanced markedly under President Mubarak , it is still very difficult for new political parties to be formed. According to the 'Parties' Law' passed under Sadat , they have to be sufficiently distinct from the existing parties and yet should not be based on religion or class (but their programme should not contradict the principles of Islamic Law); they should subscribe to the principles of national unity and social peace and to the results of popular referenda (accepting, for example, Camp David); and their programmes should not be contradictory to the principles of the July 1952 and May 1971 'revolutions' (ARE, 1984: 22-23). This is indeed an extremely tight formula, and definitely one that is capable of keeping some major (and 'real') socio-political forces - namely the Nasserists and the Muslim Brothers - out of legitimate organisation. In the absence from party competition of such popular forces, the National Democratic Party can easily claim handsome majorities, helped in this by quite a number of electioneering tricks and by the instinctive reverence for authority and fear of power among Egyptians.

The April 1987 elections were held as a result of a 'constitutional crisis' that developed towards the end of 1986, and in order that the government could pre-empt a likely decision by Egypt's relatively independent judiciary that the composition of the then existing parliament was in some respects unconstitutional. As expected, these elections saw the National Democratic Party victorious, although with fewer seats than it had gained in the 1984 elections. Of over 14 million registered voters, about half did actually vote - quite a low turnout. According to the rules, any party not obtaining in these elections some 546 thousand votes nationally would lose any seats gained locally. According to the published official reports, the National Democratic Party received about 4,752,000 (69.6 per cent); all opposition parties together obtained about 2,073,000 votes, of which about 1,164,000 (17 per cent) went to the Wafd, about 151,000 (2.21 per cent) to the Progressive Tajammu', and about 13,000 (0.19 per cent) to the minor religious party Al-Umma. These party votes translated into the following seats (excluding the 48 seats specifically allocated for 'independents'): the National Democratic Party acquired 309 seats, the Alliance with the Ikhwan took 56 seats, the Wafd gained 35 seats, and the Tajammu' and the Umma parties had no seats. Of the seats reserved for the 'independents', 40 also went to the National Democratic Party.

However, the National Democratic Party's share of seats in this election was some 60 seats fewer than it had acquired in the previous elections, while the opposition's share increased by some thirty seats. But instead of the Wafd, which formed the main opposition party in the 1984 parliament, the main opposition block is now represented by the Alliance between the Nationalistic-Islamic Labour, the Right-Wing Liberal, and the 'fundamentalist' Ikhwan (Muslim Brothers). This means that the Ikhwan, although still technically an illegal organisation, will now be substantially represented in the parliament (by 36 members including some of its most distinguished leaders) for the first time since the Revolution of 1952. The Wafd's ageing and paternalistic leadership, its wavering over secularism and its temporary alliance with Ikhwan, and its obsessive hatred of Nasser, have all perhaps started to reduce its popularity.

So the National Democratic Party has won again, even though there have been repeated accusations of rigging and corruption, including most notably those from the leader of the Wafd party , who described the election as 'the largest forgery of the people's will, and a lasting stain of shame on the forehead of the present era' (*Al-Wafd*, 8.4.1987). But even without much open rigging and corruption (although in this case there were violent skirmishes involving governmental and security 'authorities' in the working class town of Kafr al-Dawwar and elsewhere), the National Democratic Party has access to a whole organisational network - especially in the countryside - that ensures that there are proportionately more votes cast in the countryside, and that these votes 'go in the right direction'!

As with the 1984 elections, the highest turnout was in the countryside, while in Cairo the turnout was estimated at only 20 per cent; presumably those who were inclined not to support the government party, found it easier to 'vote with their feet' in Cairo, than did their counterparts who live under the tight grip of 'local government' authorities in the country.

It is partly as a result of such irregular practices that some believe the relationship between President Mubarak and the National Democratic Party (of which he is the head) to be rather uncomfortable, especially as the infitah clique continues to exploit the Party as its parliamentary façade (cf. Hirst, *The Guardian*, 8.4.1986). President Mubarak is believed to disapprove strongly of the so-called 'infitah mafia', although it is not clear whether it is merely their moral standards that he dislikes or whether he is also averse to the policies that they stand for. Some expect that the President will strike at the 'mafia' one day. Others maintain that he will always prefer to act as the arbiter rather than the orientator and commander. It remains to be seen which path President Mubarak will follow during his second presidential term.

Conclusion

It should be clear from the foregoing analysis that President Mubarak is the inheritor of a heavy, and in many ways difficult, political legacy, but that he is empowered to change that legacy in certain areas if he so desires. Although the fields of economics and foreign policy may prove particularly difficult to deal with, at least the area of 'democratisation' is largely at the disposal of the regime.

Not long after the April 1987 parliamentary elections, preparation and mobilisation for the presidential elections of October 1987 were already under way, resulting in a second term for Mubarak. There was no real competitor for President Mubarak, but the mere fact that others had dared to apply to the People's Assembly as presidential candidates is symbolically significant. The existing two-step system for presidential elections remains, however, a subject for criticism, as only one candidate is to be elected with a two-thirds majority by the People's Assembly, before being ratified by popular referendum.

Also under criticism are the existing constraints on parliamentary powers, so that, for example, a vote of no-confidence against the cabinet does not necessarily lead to its resignation, because the President may resort to a popular referendum and the dissolution of parliament. Selection of the Assembly's Speaker is still also the prerogative of the President, who may (and has done so) select for that post an MP who gained his seat in the People's Assembly through presidential appointment in the first place, rather than through popular elections.

Yet another area of criticism is the law that relates to parliamentary elections and its rigid regulations, notwithstanding its amendment for the 1987 elections. The Higher Administrative Court has actually pronounced the law unconstitutional in certain respects, and many expect the Supreme Constitutional Court to confirm this judgement. Last but not least, the Parties' Law and its applications by the Committee for Parties Affairs remain also subject to criticism; for example, when an application for a party licence by the Nasserist Arab Socialist Party was turned down, this act was also judged unconstitutional by the higher Administrative Court.

As can be seen, Egypt's relatively autonomous Courts seem to be playing a major, if technical and by definition limited, role in safeguarding the legal transformation towards political liberalisation. There are also great hopes that the President will use his significant constitutional and political powers to advance the democratisation process even further, and on a much larger scale.

Bibliography

Arab Republic of Egypt (1971), *Dustur jumhuriyyat misr al-arabiyya* [The Constitution...], Ministry of Information, Cairo.

ARE *The Yearbook: 1977*, State Information Service, Cairo.

ARE (1984) *The Political System in Egypt,* State Information Service, Cairo.

Ayubi, N. (1982 a), Implementation Capability and Political Feasibility of the Open Door Policy in Egypt in M.H. Kerr and E. S. Yassin, eds, *Rich and Poor States in the Middle East*, Westview Press, Boulder. (1982),

Ayubi, N. (1982 b), Organisation for Development: the Politico-Administrative Framework of Economic Activity in Egypt Under Sadat, *Public Administration and Development*, Vol. 2, no. 4.

Centre for Political and Strategic Studies (1986), *Al Taqrir al-istratiji al 'Arabi* [The Arab Strategic Report for 1985], CPSS, Cairo.

Ghunaim, Adil (1986), *Al-namudhaj al-misri li-ra'simaliyyat al-dawla al-tabi'a* [The Egyptian Model of Dependent State Capitalism], Dar al-Mustaqbal al-Arabi, Cairo.

Hinnebusch, Raymond (1985), *Egyptian Politics Under Sadat,* Cambridge University Press, New York.

Hilal, A., Al-Sayyid, M.K., and Badruddin, I.(1982), *Tajribat al-dimuqratiyya fi misr* [The Democratic Experience in Egypt 1970-1981], Al-Markaz al-Arabi, Cairo.

Hirst, David (1986), 'Legacy that Mubarak must Grasp', *The Guardian.* 7, 8 and 9 April.

Imam, Samia Said (1986), *Al-usul al-ijtima'iyya li nukhbat al-infitah* [Social Origins of the Infitah Elite], unpublished MSc thesis, Cairo University, Faculty of Economics and Political Science.

Mar'i, S. *et al.* (1977), *Al-dimuqratiyya fi misr* [Democracy in Egypt], Centre for Political and Strategic Studies, Cairo.

Mirel, Pierre (1982), *L'Egypte des ruptures: l'ere Sadate de Nasser Moubarak,* Sindbad, Paris

Sayid-Ahmad, Muhammad (1984), *Mustaqbal al-nizam al-hizbi fi misr* [The Future of the Party System in Egypt], Dar al-Mustaqbal al-Arabi, Cairo.

Egyptian Newspapers and Magazines.

2

THE ROLE OF THE OFFICIAL OPPOSITION

Mona Makram Ebeid

In order to provide readers with some sense of the ideological and institutional milieu within which the political opposition in Egypt has moved since 1952, we shall consider its diverse elements in the context of the major historical forces which have dominated Egyptian political life since 1952. Two major questions will be reviewed:

1. The institutional framework within which the political opposition has functioned i.e., what groups, parties, or associations exist.

2. The major issues that have concerned the opposition in parliamentary debates in the press etc.

During 1986 and the first half of 1987, Egypt experienced three major events, each of which had tremendous political implications. The police mutiny in February 1986, a constitutional crisis in December 1986, followed by the dissolution of Parliament and premature elections on 6 April, 1987. These developments are in a curious way intertwined. The police riots expressed the frustration of an important and youthful sector of the working classes with the current socio-economic policies, the constitutional crisis reflected the mounting tensions and growing demands for an expansion of the democratisation process, and President Mubarak's call for the dissolution of Parliament by referendum was motivated precisely by these serious and growing internal problems.

The first event was so serious that the army had to be called in to restore order - a dangerous precedent for any government. It also proved that the mass public, when in-system channels were closed, could make its point outside in the street, although, in the long run, this could not substitute for institutionalised mass participation. The second event was brought about when a number of advisers for the constitutional court reviewed the case filed in 1984 by lawyer Kamal Khaled to prove that the electoral law which prevented him from running for election as an independent candidate was unconstitutional (*Middle East Times* 22-28 March, April, 1987). His motion was supported by the High Administrative Court which referred his case to the Supreme Constitutional Court. Moreover, the founding member of the Nasserist Arab Socialist Party had presented an application for a party licence to the Committee on Party Law. When the Committee turned it down they also took their case to the High Administrative Council which declared the Committee's decision unconstitutional. What transpired, therefore, was that both the electoral law and the party law contained items deemed unconstitutional. It was, therefore, natural that leading members of the ruling National Democratic Party, fearing a verdict against Parliament, moved quickly to amend the current electoral law and tried to eliminate the unconstitutional items. The Committee eliminated the item which assigned a seat in each electoral district to women because it was against the constitution which calls for equal rights for all citizens in elections. Also, an item which was the source of all the furore, preventing independent candidates from running, was dropped to allow independents to run in all 48 districts, thus mixing the party-list proportional system (which dates back to 1984) and the single member constituency system (which dates back to the first elected parliament in Egypt in 1924).

In an attempt to forestall increasing opposition pressure, President Mubarak called for the dissolution of the assembly by referendum, opening the way for fresh elections on 6 April. It is important at this stage to note that this announcement occurred quite unexpectedly on 4 February, on the eve of the first-ever mass rally jointly organised long before that date by all the licensed opposition parties under the theme of 'In defence of democracy'.

Our concern here is to assess the role of the opposition forces within this structural context: a national crisis, a constitutional crisis, and a political crisis. However, before discussing the opposition in Egypt, it is necessary to consider briefly the ideological and institutional milieu within which it operates. A useful way to think about the opposition in Egypt is to consider its diverse elements in the context of the major historical forces which have dominated Egyptian political life since 1952 (Dessouki,1984 pp.32-33,44-45; Sid Ahmed, 1984).
These are:

. The Free Officers
. Revolution itself and its self-appointed heirs
. Individuals and groups who believed they represented that revolution better than did the government
. The Wafd Party, which was the major pre-revolutionary nationalist political party
. The Muslim Brotherhood, a large religious-political movement which has advocated an Islamic State and opposed secularism
. Other political forces which have existed such as the Communists, but who have not had as great an impact on the community at large

The first group can be thought of as the government, regardless of the period of time in question. The other five, including the relatively minor groups, are the opposition discussed in this paper. Rather than using a personalistic approach that would divide the post-1952 period into the Nasser period (1952-1970), the Sadat period (1970-1981), and the Mubarak period which began in 1981, another form of periodisation which would divide the 1952-1987 period into two blocks of time would provide the readers with a better sense of the political climate within which the opposition has moved since 1952.

The first period, 1952-75, was one in which a central party state apparatus (the Arab Socialist Union - ASU) became an all-encompassing system of functional representation of a new multi-class 'alliance of popular working forces'. The collapse of the monarchy had set off a power struggle in which various political forces bid for a share of power. The leaders of Egypt's veteran nationalist party, the Wafd, and those of various radical middle-class movements, by virtue of their links to the Free Officers' Movement, all made a claim. The Free Officers, however, decided not to share power but to establish an authoritarian regime. The regime monopolised all political activity and any forms of political dissent were suppressed. There was an obvious imbalance between politics and administration, and output institutions (bureaucracy, police and army) far outgrew input institutions (political parties and interest groups). The government penetrated almost all intermediary associations bringing them under its legal and financial control (Dessouki 1984). A crucial factor to the legitimacy and survival of the regime was Nasser's charismatic appeal. However, 'Nasserism' failed to institutionalise itself in an ideological party which could ensure its long-term durability or create the political instruments to mobilise and organise those social forces which favoured and benefited from Nasserism (Sid Ahmed, 1984 p.34). Ultimately, imbalance between resources and commitment, supply and demand, were to a large extent a consequence of the leader's attempt to maintain his broad nationalist popular coalition, and after the smashing defeat of 1967, the regime's coalition broke up into factions tacitly advocating contrary solutions to Egypt's crisis (Hinnebusch 1985, p. 37). Fundamental reforms seemed indispensable in order to manage growing demands for the expansion of political participation.

The second period, 1976-1987, marked the beginning of political liberalisation, primarily through a contrived multi-party system within a still presidentially dominated policy-making process (Cooper 1982, Shukri 1981). Opposition newspapers and magazines were permitted to be published. Cautious liberalisation of organised political participation as well as the reinforcement of both the press and the assembly were measures taken to balance the structural legitimacy of the regime. Nevertheless, the implementation of pluralism between 1976-1981 remained tentative, non-uniform, superficial and occasionally fictitious as the main three streams of political consciousness were prevented from being expressed openly: the Wafd, the Muslim Brethren, and the Nasserists.

President Mubarak's accession to power has allowed a legal re-emergence of the Wafd, and a tacit toleration of the two other factions, the Muslim Brethren (M.B.) and the Nasserists, through the establishment of an Egyptian variety of 'Bureaucratic - authoritarianism'. Accordingly, the authoritarian elite's political initiatives have shifted from encouraging free competition among political parties to orchestrating collaboration among economically powerful interest groups (Bianchi, 1981), and the 1984 election was a case in point. Powerful interest groups with the same socio-economic interests within the three factions represented in parliament - the ruling NDP, the Wafd and the Muslim Brethren - were working towards the establishment of a tripartite coalition, with the support of some Arab and international forces who had an interest in the emergence of a conservative social force as a strong base for the post-Sadat era (*Al Ahram*, 4 April 1987).

This period of highly controlled liberalisation of the political system, in which contrived pluralism provided an unequal channel of representation for increasingly divergent socio-economic interests, was at the base of the constitutional crisis of 1986, where demands were made for a more comprehensive system of representation along pluralist lines. Pressures to expand pluralism stem primarily from the growing demands of the political opposition for a breakthrough in the long promised, yet still elusive, transition to democracy. This involves relaxing or eliminating restrictions on the formation of parties and associations, allowing them to represent the full range of interests and ideologies in the political system, and relying on them to structure political participation through competition and collaboration in the electoral and parliamentary arenas. This summarises the bulk of the consensus which emerged among all opposition forces, legal and illegal, during the first rally held on 5 February, 1987.

The Political Opposition in Egypt

Ideologically, it would be possible to think of Egyptian political forces in conventional terms of right, left and centre, or in a slightly more complicated version: conservative, liberal, socialist, communist, fascist or anarchist. The problem is that all ideological frameworks oversimplify the Egyptian political landscape, even though they each cast some light on Egyptian politics. Furthermore, presidents do dominate the system and much of the political activity has been characterised by support for, or opposition to the president, but, interestingly, many opposition leaders have concentrated their ire on specific policies or laws and have not formulated their ideas as opposition to the president in power (Sullivan 1986, p.104). In fact, on certain issues, there seems to be a tacit consensus between the government and opposition parties. At the political level this means no normalisation of relations with Israel, and at the economic level, the maintenance of subsidies and war against corruption. Furthermore, there is a general agreement between the government and parties on the preservation of civilian rule and demilitarisation of the political process, and a recognition of the importance of Sharia law as one source, not the main source, of legislation.

Over the course of the 1952-1987 period, several major issues have been perennial highlights of Egyptian opposition politics. Some people objected to the direction of change, judging it 'too socialist' under Nasser, or 'too capitalist' under Sadat. With Mubarak, opposition figures complain that he has been too 'slow' to make decisions and that they are still; 'waiting for Mubarak' (*New York Times*, 16 May 1982). One issue which has been the most chronic of all, however, has been the demand for political freedom (*Al Ahram al-Iqtisadi*, 1984 pp.39-41). In this context, the middle class is probably the most relevant stratum in Egypt, as its members are those who staff the military, bureaucracy and schools and run both public and private sector industries. For this class, freedom of speech, press, assembly, and the right to organise groups and parties, have taken on growing significance and unite right, left and centre (Sullivan, 1986 p. 106). Although the liberty of speech and press is now well established, we will attempt to show the problems inherent in a transition to competitive democracy in Egypt. Two of these problems will be treated in this paper. First, the constraints due to the constitution, the new electoral law and party law which severely limit the scope of democracy and secondly, the very nature of the political forces in the arena seem to be a good reason for undermining the value of their contribution. In order to bring out these and other issues we will use the April elections back and forth as an illustration of the performance of these parties. But, first, a brief glance at some of the controversial provisions included in the constitution, the electoral law and the party law.

Electoral Law

In 1977, a new law permitted the formation of political parties, and in 1979, the ASU was formally abolished. Under the terms of the new Parties Law , responsibility for authorising new parties was vested in a Committee for Political Party Affairs, a part of the government whose members were appointed by the president. Unauthorised political groups in Egypt are illegal. The Parties Law of 1977 prohibits the formation of parties on the basis of religion, class , or geographical criteria.

Article 4 of Law 40/1977 is of paramount importance in decreeing which parties may or may not exist. Parties in Egypt should not be in conflict with the principles of Sharia as the principal source of legislation, the principles of the 23rd July and 15th May revolutions, the preservation of national unity, social peace, socialist gains or the democratic socialist system. In August, 1983 (Law No. 114) a new electoral law was promulgated, which amended the laws of 1972 and 1979. According to the new law, a system of proportional representation was inaugurated whereby candidates would be presented to the voters in the form of a list from each party. The electoral system works as follows. In every constituency every party proposes a list of candidates. Electoral lists may not comprise members of different parties and a vote is cast for the whole list (article 5 bis). No seats are allocated to parties not having eight per cent of the vote on the national level (article 17). Election districts were redrawn much larger than the two and three-member districts from which deputies used to be elected, and there were fewer of them: 48 election districts versus 175 districts. The number of elected seats have been increased from 390 in 1979 to 448. Thirty-one of the newly drawn districts were to have a woman candidate in addition to the male candidate, and in all districts the 50 per cent minimum proportion for membership in the Assembly of peasants and workers which was stipulated in the constitution in 1964 was to be maintained. In many instances, however, 'worker' or 'peasant' status was more formal than real and reflected more about what the individuals were than what they are, thus allowing for many 'legal' irregularities.

The constitution allows the president to appoint ten members. The ten appointed members are supposed to include some individuals of distinction, especially from the non-political world. This device was instituted by President Nasser to enable him to appoint distinguished (but loyal) members of the Christian Copts to parliament, as very few Copts have ever won office in parliament. By law, voting is mandatory but not all adults are registered to vote. Furthermore, while the law stipulates that men must register and vote, women are free to do so but are not similarly obliged.

The rigid regulations found in the constitution as well as the party and electoral laws have severely limited the scope of democracy in Egypt, and it is no wonder that all parties without exception have given pride of place to constitutional reform. The constitutional crisis of this year is only one aspect of the strained tensions between government and opposition that have characterised parliamentary life since the last elections in 1984. Thus, although the regime has made way to allow limited participation of independents (48), to contest parliamentary elections in a bid to restore credibility to parliament, opposition leaders insist that the law is still unconstitutional, and indeed, many analysts regard the controversy of the constitutionality of the law as having serious repercussions on the ability of the legislature to do business for some time (*Middle East Times*, 1-7 March, 1987). More than the constitutional irregularities of the law, it is the political aspect which seems more meaningful in this respect, that is, the provisions of the electoral law make it far too difficult and even impossible to have a wide range of opinions being expressed, while at the same time allowing the ruling party to get a majority and limitless continuity. Consequently, the ruling party has been characterised by what seems a monolithic representation of the elite over the past three decades. Thus, the Free Officers, the members of the ASU, or those of the NDP represent a kind of 'unanimism', leaving little room for the expression of 'counter elites', as appeared in the bloody confrontation between the M.B. and the Nasserist regime (1954), and in the difficulties encountered by the democratic experience under the multi-party system installed by Sadat when confronted by the Wafd (1978).

The Parties

There are six official political parties in Egypt. These are: the National Democratic Party (Al Hizb al Watani al Dimuqrati - to which we shall refer as the NDP), the New Wafd (Hizb al Wafd al Jadid), the Socialist Labour Party (Hizb al Amal al Ishtraki - hereafter referred to as the SLP), the Nationalist Unionist Progressive Party (Hizb al Tagammu' al Watani al Taqaddumi - hereafter referred to as NUPP), the Liberal Party (Hizb al Ahrar), and the Umma Party.

The New Wafd

Although the other parties, to some degree, were created by the regime, the New Wafd was a revival of the pre-revolutionary Wafd. The Chairman of the party, Fouad Serag El Din, a former Minister of the Interior under Farouk, held the post of Secretary-General when the 'old' Wafd was made illegal in 1954. In February 1978, soon after the changes in the law in 1977, the Wafd resurrected itself. It turned out to be a potent rival of the government party for the loyalties of the bourgeoisie , and a magnet for diverse elements seeking an alternative to the regime but sympathetic neither to the left nor to Islamic fundamentalism (Ansari 1986). It lasted only '100 Days' before it ceased political activity, charging that harassment from the Sadat regime made it impossible for the New Wafd to continue. In fact, many political analysts consider the episode of the Wafd's first re-emergence and sudden demise as an example of the limits that have been set on the multi-party system from the start, by keeping all the reins of power in the leader's hand, and by miscalculating how far liberalisation was to go (Reed 1978 p.391). Its emergence had also been part of a far-reaching attempt to come to grips with both the Nasser era and the pre-1952 period, and to set a course for the future. In any case, after a long court case, the Wafd was allowed to resume its activities in 1983.

As the legitimate heir to the old Wafd - the veteran party of nationalist politics, coupled with a secular tradition - the party attracted at one point an important number of Copts , in addition to its constituency amid the rural middle class and urban liberal professions, mainly lawyers and judges. However, the electoral alliance between the New Wafd and the M.B. in 1984 disquieted a number of secular Wafdists. A split in the party occurred, with many prominent Wafdist members, such as historian Mohammed Anis, and the well-known literary critic, Louis Awad, leaving the party with fracas, arguing that the Wafd's inability to stand fast on its secular principles undermined everything it had originally fought for. Other dissenters included a young consultant agronomist, Farag Ali Foda, who still insists on the need for a secular party and who has written several books virulently attacking the 'sacralisation' of politics by the Islamist trend (Foda 1983). Since then he has relentlessly asked for a licence to establish an independent liberal secular party, Al Mustaqbal, but permission was refused. (He stood for election in 1986 as an independent but did not win.) However, it is worthy of note, in view of the recent developments, that the Islamic trend within the Wafd was far from extremist. Umar el Telmessani, the Supreme Guide then, made it clear in one of his articles published in *Al Wafd* newspaper, that what the M.B. hoped was that the Wafd would be the 'first party to apply the law of God, or if not, then support those who want to. Should the party insist on socialism then let it be Islamic Socialism which is more precise, complete and profitable' (*Al Wafd*, 22.3.1984). He added that the problem with the Wafd is that it wants 'to please all voters' (*Al Wafd*, 22.3.1984). That is still its problem. At first it appealed to the Coptic vote with promises of secularisation, then it called on the M.B. to join it, promising them a Sharia -based state. After the departure of the M.B. this year from its ranks, and in a bid to re-establish its traditionally secular image, the party leader overtly declared that it was against the formation of parties based on religion (*Al Wafd*, March 1987). This, however, failed to trigger the expected support of Christian Egyptians whose spiritual leaders seemed convinced that their interests lay more with the government party, the NDP.

As one sees in their programme, the Wafd has joined the opposition in calling for legal reforms, notably the freedom of association for all political parties, a reform of the eight per cent law and the choosing of the President and Vice President by direct universal suffrage. Based on the right-wing of the civilian bourgeoisie and chiefly anti-statist in orientation, it called for a more thorough economic liberalisation and a political one to match it. One final point in which the Wafd is similar to the opposition is in its foreign policy: the party thus calls for cancelling the Camp David Agreement as the latter has been repeatedly violated by Israel, notably over Taba and Palestinian rights of self-determination. Apart from its credibility in championing individual liberties and democracy, the Wafd's programme, despite its posturing as the largest and most ancient opposition party, seems to be in agreement with basic government policy but keen to change the rules of the electoral game to allow itself a place in the sun. An interview, which took place in 1983, between Fouad Serag El Din and the Minister of the Interior, explicitly summarises the vision that the party leader harboured for his party. He stated that his vision of future political life in Egypt was an alternation of two large parties British style. The NDP and the New Wafd were; 'two strong and basic parties having enough self-confidence to enable them to pursue the democratic path far from the provocation to which some segments of the petty opposition might resort' (*Al Missawar*, 23 September, 1983). A similar position was adopted in 1987, underlining the same attitude. A plan had been agreed by all leaders of the opposition parties at their mass rally, after President Mubarak issued his decree calling for a referendum on dissolving parliament, to unify all opposition party lists into one single list under the umbrella of the Wafd in a co-ordinated move against the National Democratic Party (NDP). However, the plan was short-lived as the Wafd Party's High Council turned down the idea on the grounds of illegality and opted instead for a purely Wafdist list. Interestingly, the Wafd leader had favoured the idea, as he saw in a joint list a prospect of the Wafd taking the splinter parties under its wing and standing on an equal footing with the ruling NDP. It was the Wafd's deputy leader, a prominent legal expert, who said that the electoral law unmistakably forbids joint party lists and thus they will present their own list (*Al Wafd*, February 12, 1987).

In the recent election, the Wafd were able to field slate listed candidates in 46 out of 48 constituencies, and 37 candidates for independent seats. This did not prevent them from suffering a severe setback. They only managed to win eleven per cent of the votes (36 seats) compared to 15 per cent in 1984 (58 seats). The set-back in elections was not only the result of government attacks and interference in elections, rival parties competition and the impediments posed by the electoral law; the party would have been more effective if it had avoided its embarassing and debilitating internal struggles. Over the past three years seventeen members have dissented. Furthermore, lack of effective grassroot organisation, based on a more realistic approach to the social and economic changes which have transformed Egypt's political landscape over the past three decades, have prevented it from harnessing its real but diffuse support.

The main themes which run through its newspaper, *Al Wafd*, are: the almost golden age before 1952, the black record of the Nasser regime, the apalling catalogue of current Egyptian problems and the hope for a better age under a liberal parliamentary government. Such themes tended to be attractive to an important segment of the population when it first re-emerged but three or four years later they sound redundant, particularly as they are unaccompanied by a new ideological mix which could galvanize the imagination of the young. Consequently, it is portrayed as the Party of the Elders, particularly since the internal structural inconsistencies prevent the projection of an eager and enthusiastic second stratum. Furthermore, the fluidity of its programme does not singularise it from other parties. In the past it had been known as the party of the revolutionary nationalist bourgeoisie which attracted wide sectors of the nationalist elements from a broad cross-class coalition.

In raising doubts about official policies during parliamentary debates the Wafd had considerable impact on the educated public opinion, as well as relentlessly exposing government corruption and mismanagement and on pushing for a freer parliament. If it can solve its identity crisis by projecting a clear socio-economic programme of reform, it could still rally great support from many Egyptians who see in it a credible means of winning a freer press, personal liberties and a truly multi-party democracy.

The Socialist Labour Party (SLP)

The party was founded in 1978 by Sadat, and was put under the leadership of his brother-in-law, Mahmoud Abou Wafia, to become a 'loyal opposition' to the NDP. The party, however, escaped Sadat's control and has become a revival of the 'Young Egypt' fascist party of the 1940s. Its programme has changed little since that time (Vatikiotis,1978, pp. 30, 67-84). It is led by Ibrahim Shukri and Fathy Radwan, both old members of Young Egypt. The new Editor-in-Chief of their party newspaper, Adel Hussain, recently elected to the Central Committee, is a relation of Ahmed Hussein, the founder of the Young Egypt movement. Helmy Murad, the Secretary General of the party, is his brother-in-law, and his own son, Magdy Ahmed Hussain, won a seat in the People's Assembly in April, 1987.

The party is intensely nationalistic and religious , two facts which, as we shall see later, have facilitated a 'coalition' with the M.B. during the recent elections. In fact, many observers have described this coalition, or 'alliance', as an M.B. takeover of the party, and several questions are now being raised as to the future of the SLP (*Al Yom al Sabah*, 6 April, 1987). The motto of the party is 'Allah and the People'. During the elections and under the impact of the new M.B. coalition it was changed to Allah Akbar. The inside of the cover of the party programme in 1984 admits its connection with 'Young Egypt' and the 'Socialist Party' as a means of legitimising the party. The party is against 'consumerist' Infitah for moral rather than economic reasons (Wahba, 1984) and supports 'productive Infitah'. The Azhar's position in the Arab and Islamic world is to be upheld and the aim of political life is the creation of the United Arab States through a development of the Arab League. No mention is made of Israel although the party is anti Camp David, which it had accepted 'with reservations' in 1979 and now refutes. The party calls for social justice by indexing wages and pensions to the cost of living and a progressive fiscal system.

It is interesting to note that in the 'coalition' programme of this year no mention is made of 'social justice', a term closely connected to leftist jargon, although the stipulation on wages and pension was the same. Also, no mention is made of the United Arab States or the Arab League. Instead, there is a clause stipulating that Egyptian national security requires Arab complementarity and co-operation with Islamic states in every domain, and there is support for the Palestinian struggle, all being linked to the 'freezing of the Camp David Accords', paving the way for its abrogation. Non-alignment between East and West is considered necessary for Islamic renaissance, and Zionism is mentioned as 'our most dangerous enemy'. Finally, preferential relations, whether economic or military, with the U.S. are refused. (*Al Shaab*, 6 April, 1987).

The 'coalition' with the M.B. and the Liberal party is viewed not only as 'a necessity to overcome the electoral law's limits on representation' and the party law's restriction on 'the formation of parties'; it was described by the spokesman of the party, Adel Hussain, as a desirable alliance and not an electoral strategy because of ideological similarities towards the common ultimate aim, which is the establishment of an Islamic state (*Al Shaab*, March,1987).

The incipient crisis conditions which have characterised the SLP during the past three years, due on the one hand to the lack of an organisational infrastructure for a national campaign, and on the other hand to factional tensions within the party between the socialist democratic wing and the more fundamentalist wing, became exacerbated during the elections. A number of the elected leadership resigned. Some joined the NDP (Sayed Rustum), others decided to fight the leadership through legal means. This team was headed by one of their most prominent leaders, Aboul Fadlal Guizawy, a lawyer who has raised a legal case against the unconstitutionality of the alliance. (Art. 5 of the electoral law stipulates that electoral lists may not comprise members of different parties.) Moreover, sixty of its members, at the behest of two members of the High Executive Committee, held a meeting in Cairo during the elections and passed resolutions whereby the party leader was to be held accountable for infringement of the party principles by agreeing to the alliance, and gave a free hand to the M.B. to position their candidates prominently on the party lists. They also demanded that a general conference of the party be held after the elections, with the prerogative of withdrawing confidence from the party leader and exposing to public opinion the infringement of the party leadership by the socialist democratic lines of the party (*Al Ahali*, March, 1987).

The initial event which triggered the crisis was the predominance of major M.B. leaders topping the lists in more than twenty districts. Prominent among these were Seif al-Islam Hassan al-Banna (son of the founder), Mahmoud el Hodeiby (son of another leader) and Salah Abu Ragik, the latter two, leaders of the former secret apparatus of the organisation. Furthermore, the M.B. had succeeded in preventing the enlistment of the Nasserists and Marxist elements of the SLP. Simultaneously, the theoriser and leader of the Jihad organisation (one of the radical Islamist groups), Dr. Omar Abdel Rahman, unexpectedly announced his support of the alliance. In view of the election results, where the M.B. won 35 out of the 56 seats allotted to the 'alliance', and considering their marked predominance on the political scene, the future of the SLP itself is being questioned (*Al Yom al Sabah*, 16 March).

The Nationalist Unionist Progressive Party (NUPP)

This party was formed in 1976 as the manifestation of the left tendency of the Arab Socialist Union. In press reports it is often described as a marginal group of Marxist and left-wing Nasserist intellectuals together with some trade unionists (Hendricks, 1982). However, the characterisation of the NUPP as a marginal political club of leftist intellectuals tends to undermine its potential as a force in the political arena. The party is headed by Khaled Muhy Eddin, a former member of the Revolutionary Command Council, who split with Nasser over the 1954 events. The picture that emerges from a fairly recent study on the legal left (Hendricks, 1982) in Egypt, indicates that the main recruiting ground and base of support is found among socially mobile people of modest background (sons of workers or sons of peasants). These people work in public sector industry and/or government administrations, the majority of the active members being recruited from the ranks of the lower level muwazzafin (white collar employees), what Abdel Fadil calls, following Poulantzas, 'the new petit bourgeoisie ...consisting of white collar employees, technicians, line supervisors and civil servants' (Abdel Fadil, 1975, p.94). It was this layer of society that had constituted the popular base of the Nasser regime in the urban areas (Hendricks, 1982, p.52).

One of the main problems the party faces is directly related to the constraints of the party law. Since the regime have decided on allowing only one left party - preferably a purely communist one, so as to marginalise it more easily - and in particular have prevented the creation of an independent Nasserist party, many oppositional Nasserists, Arab Nationalists and National Democratic personalities have joined the NUPP. This, of course, has meant the uneasy co-existence of different political tendencies, and the necessity for compromise solutions, often in conflict with the needs of militant members who want clear-cut programmes, particularly on social and class issues, and a clean political line. Persistent harassment by the government in the past, branding it as communist and atheist, in a region where religious feeling is very sensitive, has prevented its growth. Again, this is one area which always causes the party to be on the defensive and to announce from time to time that its leader is away in Saudi Arabia on an omra, the small pilgrimage. Many of the leading articles, in times of communal tension particularly, try to give a progressive interpretation of Islam, bringing out the basic compatibility of Islamic principles with socialism. This has not prevented them in the last elections from being the target of attack by the 'coalition'. One question raised by the Supreme Guide, Hamed Aboul Nasr, during the elections was; 'Is it permissible that the atheists are allowed a party and the believers are not?' (*Al Ahrar*, March, 1987). Yet, the NUPP had constantly pressed for the freedom of party formation to be extended to all political forces including the M.B. In its response to repeated attacks for its 'incompatibility' with Islam, and within the context of its refusal to join the 'coalition', the Secretary of the Central Committee replied that it was not ready to abandon its principles of national unity for a handful of seats in parliament (*Al Ahali*, March 1987). Having no elected representative in parliament, and being unable to hold public meetings or official rallies, except within their headquarters, further isolates local provincial committees from their heartland. The main weapon for confronting government attacks and for criticising, often virulently, government policies, has been the party's weekly newspaper, *Al Ahali* (150,000 copies which, by Egyptian standards, is a reasonable number).

Interestingly, the relaxation of restrictions on the Nasserists in 1987, allowing them to publish their own newspaper, *Sawt al Arab* as well as permission to convene their first conference, has seriously weakened the all-embracing leftist front which the NUPP has traditionally stood for since 1976. A number of important members of the Central Committee and the General Secretariat moved to the Nasserist party as founding members. Simultaneously, the Marxists outside the party have relentlessly asked for a licence for the Egyptian Communist Party to operate. With this in mind, a number of them have stood for elections as independents and not on the NUPP slate, hoping to win a few independent seats. Prominent among them was Dr. Nabil al-Hilaly, one of the main figures of the pre-1952 Communist Party. In the recent election the NUPP failed to win any seats and its percentage of votes decreased from four per cent in 1984 to two per cent.

According to A. Bahaa El Din, a respected independent columnist in *Al Ahram*, the NUPP Tagammu' had such a result because it dropped the ideological mix which had traditionally attracted leftist groupings (*M.E.T.*, 19-25 April, 1987). The greatest surprise to everyone was the defeat of its leader, Khaled Mohyeddin, who, although declared winner in the first announcement of results, found out he was not winner in the second round - a familiar scenario!

The Liberal Party

Developed from one of the ASU original 'platforms', it was headed by Mustafa Kamel Murad, a second rank Free Officer. It has changed its name with the unofficial relaxation of controls on party positions from the Liberal Socialists to the Liberal Party. Despite its declared attachment to basic liberties, the party is fiercely fundamentalist and owns one of the most virulent anti-Christian newspapers, *Al Nur*, in addition to its party organ, *Al Ahrar*. Due to an almost total depletion of its party leadership, as some of its most prominent members have left it, including the head of its Parliamentary caucus (Olfat Kamel), to join the Wafd, it has recently taken a more fundamentalist approach in order to attract M.B. dissenters from the Wafd. Consequently, Salah Abu Ismail, a well-known fundamentalist, joined the party as Secretary General. He stood for election as an independent and won the Giza seat. Eager to participate in the elections, the LP joined the 'alliance' with twenty per cent of candidates allotted to it. Interestingly, the party leader did not run for election. He had previously been appointed at the *Majlis al-Shura*, the second chamber, in October 1986, breaking ranks with the opposition, which had decided to boycott elections and refuse appointments.

The Umma Party

Size-wise this is indeed a 'petty' opposition, with no programme and hardly any members. It campaigned at the recent elections for the Sharia as the basic source of all laws. To the surprise of everyone, it managed to acquire 13,000 votes nation-wide, amounting to 0.5 per cent. It is headed by Ahmed el Sabahy, a former school teacher.

The April 6th Elections: Future Prospects

April 6th 1987 saw the second multi-party election to be held in less than three years. During four weeks, Egypt was practising its own brand of democracy, with six parties holding rallies and meetings across the country. Having participated myself at them as a Wafdist candidate, I would like to share with you some of my impressions regarding the results and future prospects of Egypt's democratic experience. What follows is brief and is not intended to be a comprehensive analysis of the recent elections. It is included in order to provide you with some sense of the ideological and institutional milieu within which the elections have taken place.

While the apportionment of seats in the People's Assembly does not reflect the real balance of forces in the country, the tally of votes for the 1987 elections helps to shed light on the dynamics of opposition politics in Egypt. Fifteen thousand candidates contested 400 seats on the proportional list system and 398 independents contested the 48 seats allotted to them. The published figures revealed that the opposition managed to win 95 seats out of 448 seats in parliament, according to several writers, the biggest ever number since the beginning of parliamentary life in 1924. Equally important is that despite an intensive campaign prior to the April poll, in which the opposition parties held 467 electoral meetings and the independent candidates 268 meetings, the election turnout was still low. According to official announcements, only 54 percent of the registered voters (14.3 million) cast their votes.

Personally, I would tend to think that only forty per cent went to the polls, as the present electoral list includes three million Egyptians living abroad and two and a half million who have died. The remainder is nine million voters out of which barely four million went to the polls. An indication of this fact is that according to official figures the largest turnout was in rural Egypt, while in Cairo, presumably the most literate, sophisticated and politicised area of the country, vote turnout was only 30 per cent (10 per cent less than in 1984). Voter apathy may be at the heart of low turnout as well as cynicism due to past political experience. From 1952-1977 Egyptians were ruled by the single party system and since then by one big party. The result is that people still feel that political balance is already calculated ahead of time in favour of a given party, and all that the other parties can do is to improve the position of the minority in face of the fixed majority. A variety of additional reasons lie behind this indifference, including the worries of living conditions, the lack of political consciousness due to a high rate of illiteracy (70 per cent), the loss of hope in the possibility of change and the lack of faith in the relevancy of the political party system to meet their needs. The seriousness of this phenomenon is that such apathy gives rise to segments of the population, who tend to become the monopoly of political and social trends outside the scope of the political parties, with the result that their future political action cannot be determined due to the absence of channels between them and the parties. A recent sociological study has found that the actual political system did not amount to more than an adjustment in the political superstructure which has existed during the past three decades, with the counter-effect that class consciousness and political consciousness in Egyptian society were much weaker than they were before the Revolution (NRCC: 1986, p.247).

One of the enigmas of the elections was the sizeable number of 'spoiled' votes (402,559 out of 7,227,467 votes cast) giving rise to what many called 'the spoiled ballot party' (*Middle East Times*, 19-25 April, 1987). In the previous election spoiled votes totalled 181,542, thus a 122 per cent increase in the recent ones.

The national vote by party:

May 1984

Party	Votes (%)	Seats
NDP	72.9	389
NWP	15.1	59
(inc. M.B.)		(8)
SLP	7.1	-
NPURP	4.2	-
		448
Nominated by President		10
Total		<u>458</u>

April 1987

Party	Votes (%)	Seats on party slates	Independents
NDP	69.6	309	40
SLP (alliance)	17.0	56	4
(inc. M.B.)		36	
NWP	10.9	35	-
NPURP	2.21	-	-
Umma	0.19	-	-
Independents	-	-	(4)
		400	48
Nominated by President		10	
		<u>Total 458</u>	

Note: Among the seats on party slates (400), workers represent 160 deputies and peasants 63 deputies, amounting to approximately 26 per cent. All the independent seats had NDP support.

- No left representative, either from the NUPP or independent Marxists or Nasserists won a seat
- 14 women compared to 32 in 1984 obtained seats this year, suggesting a more conservative trend

- No Coptic independent won a seat, 5 out of 7 on the NDP succeeded and 1 on the 'alliance' ticket in Assiut, as the Supreme Guide of the M.B., Hamed Aboul Nasr supported his candidacy.
- Ten candidates were appointed by the President to make up for electoral 'imbalances': 4 women, among them 2 Copts; 2 Copts; 4 personalities, prominent among them being the Head of Al Azhar.

Beyond the characteristic complaints about the legitimacy of the election procedure, the most dominant factor in the poll has been the political salience and unprecedented prominence of the M.B., theoretically banned from party politics. Unable to form a party of their own, due to the restrictive party law and the rigid conditions of the electoral law (stipulating an eight per cent limit for parties to qualify for representation), the M.B. struck a deal with the Labour and Liberal parties whereby they be allowed to field 40 per cent of candidates, Labour another 40 and the Liberals 20 per cent, thus managing a significant, albeit oblique assault on legislative power. There is no official figure for the M.B. votes in the election. However, some mathematical approximations might be indicative: the alliance won 1,163,525 votes. In the 1984 elections the SLP and the LP won 834,311 votes. The difference is 329,214 votes, which may roughly approximate the M.B. vote strength this time. Officially, the tally states that 38 seats go to M.B., 16 to Labour and 6 to LP, a result which prompted the Wafd to announce that it would challenge the decision that the alliance leads the opposition, on the grounds that it received more seats than the SLP and that the M.B. has no right to be represented as it has no legal status. Although they have indirectly participated in the last legislative elections in 1984, the M.B. performance this time differed both quantitatively and qualitatively from 1984. Out of 500 candidates fielded by the Wafd in 1984, the M.B. had 40 and only eight won seats (*Al Ahram*, 4 April, 1987). They never had a common programme with the Wafd and the political discourse during and after elections was mostly secular in essence, in keeping with Wafdist guidelines, and thus their call for the implementation of Sharia showed many signs of pragmatism. Through the Wafd opposition in parliament, the moderate elements of the Islamic constituency were permitted to participate in legislative debates and to declare that their goal was to press for the gradual adoption and application of the Sharia as a prerequisite for the establishment of an Islamic state. It was this gradualist orientation which the late Supreme Guide, Omar el Telmessani, advocated as constituting the basic socio-political line of the M.B. This time they were running one hundred candidates and the issue of Islamic law became central to the campaign of the 'alliance', with political discourse entirely couched in religious terms. One side effect has been that the two smaller parties, Labour and the Liberals, who last time failed to breach the eight per cent limit of the popular vote necessary to win seats, this time were pushing their Islamic credentials to the detriment of any other issue. With the support of enormous financial resources, the M.B. managed a massive deployment of posters and banners covering all the walls of the cities, provinces and villages. Their publicity campaign was mainly geared to attract the ordinary man's strong sentimentality for the Islamic message. They presented themselves, in fact, as the representatives of the community of believers, not as a community of believers (*Al Yom al Sabah*, 6 April, 1987), and filled the street with a brief slogan 'Islam is the solution' (Al Islam huwwa al hall), trying to instill in the ordinary Muslim voters the feeling that giving the M.B. their vote was tantamount to the Shihada and that it was their duty to vote for those who will shoulder the responsibility (and Jihad) for the implementation of Islamic Sharia , in order that it becomes the only source of legislation. The implication being that with faith in God all problems will be resolved. Other slogans read; 'Give your vote to God, give to the Muslem Brotherhood'. Still others made it clear that giving votes to the government was equal to giving them to the devil (*Middle East Times*, 6 April). The banners, on the other hand, carried the M.B. credo 'God is our objective, the Prophet our leader and the Koran our Constitution'.

The widespread Islamic fervour being injected into the campaign triggered wide-ranging debates and varied reactions across the political spectrum, the following being the most salient:

First, the Government reacted after the campaign was entering its last week by threatening to remove all such posters, charging that the M.B. was still banned and thus had no legal right to put posters anywhere. The M.B. claimed, on the other hand, that the constitution gave them the right to run for election as religious individuals, if not as a political party (*Middle East Times*, 5-11 April).

Secondly, great concern arose among several secular Egyptian liberals, both Copts and Muslims. The wave of communal violence between Muslims and Christians in several towns and villages of Upper Egypt during the electoral campaign jolted political and intellectual leaders, and set off a series of articles by Egyptian writers calling for action by the Muslim majority. A consensus had emerged that the Copt's isolation and passivity in political life was increasingly serving as a hotbed of dissent that could threaten the country's national unity. Already, some Copts in Assiut, a centre of Muslim-Christian tension, had announced the formation of the 'Christian Jihad', as opposed to the Islamic Jihad organisation. As a result, in a joint move by Islamic and Christian intellectual figures, a conference was convened to discuss ways of promoting national unity. Stepped up declarations of brotherly love on both sides - traditionally a standard part of political theory - filled the newspapers, but no consensus was reached on where non-Muslims fitted into the society. The most bitter article, though, came from leftist Christian journalist, Maged Atteya, in *Al Ahali* of 25th March, where he attributed Copts' non-participation in public life to the fanaticism that prevailed in the country. Others saw that it was difficult to prevent sporadic incidents of violence against the Copts and that the government may have seen the Copts as a convenient safety valve or 'scapegoat' for releasing the frustrations of the masses due to the acute economic crisis (Ibrahim, 1984). Wafdist reaction was interesting; realising that they were facing a formidable competitor, who might score more than them in the elections and thus deprive them of the leadership of opposition in parliament, they declared that the M.B. was manipulating religious symbols in a quest for power and not religiosity (*Al Wafd*, Wahid Raafat, March, 1987). Leftist intellectuals, in both government and opposition papers, saw that the real challenge was between those who wanted the prevalence of laws derived from the Constitution against those who favoured laws derived from God.

Thirdly, amid all the flurry, the President came out with several statements emphasising the importance of national unity for the stability of the country, adding that there would be no amendment to the constitution, thus cutting short demands from both Wafdists (for a new liberal constitution) and from the M.B.(for a new religious constitution).

The new expanding role of the M.B. is sure to pose a serious challenge to the future of the nation's democratic experiment. Several factors over the past years have contributed to deepen what is felt as a pervading crisis situation. These factors may be categorised under five headings.

1. A Deepening Economic Crisis

Egypt's most demanding medium-term challenge is clearly economic. This would involve a greater emphasis on comprehensive economic planning and on the often unpopular allocation of differential benefits and sacrifices to various social and economic categories. The 'middling' classes - small shopkeepers, students, artisans, clerks, teachers and civil servants - have been hard hit by the high rate of inflation as a result of the state's economic policies. Opportunities for upward mobility have decreased and developments like the trimming of the public sector, the calling into question of free education and guaranteed jobs for graduates, have made it increasingly difficult for this stratum to retain its socio-economic status. These economic frustrations have been compounded by the emergence of a new, affluent, commercial elite in the private sector, who are prominent in business and government, and who seek political representation. President Mubarak has taken action against some conspicuous instances of corruption but his government seems unable, or unwilling, to offer a viable alternative to Infitah policies to ameliorate the economic situation. In fact, what transpired during the elections regarding the NDP was that it seemed that the President had more opposition inside his own party to some of his own ambitions than from the opposition itself. To that end, he is trying to carve himself a 'centrist' coalition away from the still influent Sadatist coterie and a weak leftist faction.

2. A Contrived Political Liberalisation

While initially a relative tolerance of political expression has allowed competing tendencies to exist, pressures continue to accumulate for greater structural coherence along pluralist democratic lines which would require a substantial broadening of the elite. The government's efforts, however, to divert public discourse from political reform result in sharpening the conflicting demands they seek to resolve or contain.

3. Impotence at the Foreign Policy Level

The failure of the regime to forge a relationship with Israel which would satisfy large segments of Egyptian public opinion - which would entail making serious efforts to establish a Palestinian entity guaranteeing self-determination for the Palestinian people.

4. Social Inconsistencies

The sporadic wave of communal violence which Egypt has witnessed in recent years is a reaction to the deepening crisis that pervades the region. Government policies, in that instance, have been marked by an odd combination of sensitivity, uncertainty, inaction and reluctant decisiveness. Only when events such as the outbreak of recent confrontations occur, are peoples consciences stirred and everyone is enthusiastically geared to national unity. It still remains a fact that without a commitment to equality and citizenship rights, it would be difficult for the regime to retain the loyalty of a minority (the Copts) no longer certain of its place in a shifting society and often prone out of insecurity to retreat to communalism, on the basis that if they could not be genuinely equal, then they would have to work towards a position that would grant them safety through separation.

5. Atrophy of the Political Parties

Apart from a lively opposition press which has helped to check some of the most audacious 'smash and grab' efforts of influent pressure groups at the expense of the public or the poor (such as the Pyramid plateau, Cairo Zoo, slum clearance and other cases), all opposition parties lack the political infrastructure needed to aggregate mass opinion into the policy process. Lack of political groundwork and the inability to offer a new vision of hope and inspiration has prompted a perceptive analyst of the political scene to call it the 'Democracy of one million citizens' (*Al Ahram*, 3.11.1986), thus questioning the relevance of the entire political system regarding the majority of the Egyptian people.

Conclusion

By the year 2000, Egypt will have approximately 70 million inhabitants. Because of insufficient job creation, they are likely to be poorer than today's Egyptians. The only way out is by sharing wealth more equitably. If present trends continue, in all likelihood the opposite will happen. This is not inevitable, although it will be exceedingly difficult to avoid. But achieving a better distribution of the country's wealth is now probably a more important political task than creating newer and greater wealth. If something has to give, it could be the Egyptian political system. But it must change at the worst possible time under the worst possible circumstances of no growth or jobs and with fewer subsidies and of more inequality as well as a surge of violence mainly against the state.

One of the main reasons advanced by several analysts is that the system cannot survive a true liberalisation of the economy, as an open economy necessarily implies an open political arena. The former is going forward while the latter is not moving fast enough. The reason for this link is quite simple. Ever since the establishment of a state-controlled economy in the 1950s, one of the key characteristics of the political system has been the so-called push-button economy. Like everywhere else - the U.S. included -

the Egyptian state, implying essentially the President and his close entourage, has been able to use the principal levers of the country's economy for political purposes. But in Egypt this practice has been much more extensive: as a means of control, coercion, redistribution and bureaucratic authoritarianism. When a subsidy or irrigation project or highway is necessary it is so decided and implemented. If an industry or a political faction has to be protected from foreign competition, import quotas or other restrictions are immediately imposed. Conversely, if political enemies have to be destroyed, co-opted or cajoled, the country's leaders can resort to a number of economic policy instruments to do what is necessary: new investment or credit cut-offs, higher salaries or lower ones, price freezes or increases. A system that has depended on a push-button economy, as Egypt did for the past three decades, is now reaping the results of an uncontrolled open door policy: there are many fewer buttons to push. Economic and financial flows, wages, prices and jobs are no more subject to the proverbial 'blind forces of the market' than anywhere else, but the government's control of them is diminishing considerably.

Co-optation, protection, subsidies and public investment are no longer available as political tools. This is what is seriously hampering the political system's treatment of those who lose out within it or who are excluded from it. Consequently, movements of protest have taken a new form of mobilisation during the last decades of the 20th century: Islam-based politics. The latter expresses at once an assertion of a personal and collective identity and the desire for autonomy from foreign imperialism - which is felt as cultural aggression and material exploitation - and what is more important, a revolt against the state which is seen as manipulative, corrupt and corrupting.

Although there is wide agreement that the political system must change, great emphasis has been placed by all the opposition parties on the electoral aspect of the change that is needed. But there is a glaring lack of basic democratic processes in Egypt's labour unions, news media and in the bureaucracy as well. Pressure to expand pluralism stems primarily from the growing demands of the political opposition for a breakthrough in the long promised yet still elusive transition to democracy. This would involve relaxing or eliminating restrictions on the formation of parties and associations, allowing them to represent the full range of interests and ideologies in the political system, and relying on them to structure political participation through competition and collaboration in the electoral and parliamentary elections. Many Egyptians today have a stake in social tranquility and political continuity, and it is possible for any faction or politician to find fertile ground for rebellion or radical breaks with the status quo. Quite possibly nothing would happen if there were elections with several contending parties and even candidates for the Presidency. There is no guarantee, of course, that losers would not attempt to overturn the results in the streets. But there is little likelihood that many Egyptians would support such an endeavour.

The difficulty lies in convincing those in power to create conditions whereby they may lose it. For only with change at the very top will Egypt's democratisation go beyond electoral matters to extend into all realms of society. And only then will it gain the support of Egypt's 'silent majority'.

Bibliography

Books

Abdel Fadil, M. (1975), *Development, Income Distribution and Social Change in Rural Egypt* (1952-1970); Cambridge, Cambridge University Press

Ansari, H, (1986), *Egypt, The Stalled Society*, State University of New York Press

Cooper, M. (1982), *The Transformation of Egypt;* Croom Helm, London

Foda, F. (1983), *On Secularism;* Dar el Arabi, Cairo

Hinnebusch, R. (1985), *Egyptian Politics under Sadat;* Cambridge, Cambridge University Press

Sid Ahmed, M. (1984), *The Future of the Party System in Egypt;* Dar el Mustaqbal al Arabi, Cairo

Shukri, G. (1981), *Egypt: Portrait of a President*; Zed Press

Sullivan, E.L. (1986), *Women in Egyptian Public Life;* Syracuse University Press

Vatikiotis, P.J. (1978), *Nasser and His Generation*; St. Martin's Press, New York

Articles

Bianchi, R. (1981), *Interest Representation in Modern Egypt* (unpublished paper) American University in Cairo

Dessouki, A.H., (1984), *The Future of Parties in Egypt ,Ruz al Yusuf,* pp. 32, 33, 44-45

New York Times, *'Waiting for Mubarak'*, 16 May, 1982

Ibrahim, Saad Eddin, *Spring of Fury, Al Ahram al Iqtisadi,* 2 May, 1984

Kholy, L., *Democracy of a Million Citizens, Al Ahram,* November, 1986

Reid, Dohaed M. *The Return of the Egyptian Wafd,* 1978, Int. Journal of African Historical Studies, 1979, 12 (3), 389-415

Heindriks, B. (1982), *The Legal Left: A Cairo Case Study,* Middle Eastern Studies, University of Amsterdam

N.R.C.C. (1986), (National Research Center Criminology), *Egypt; A Global Social Survey of Egyptian Society* (1952-1980)

Wahba, M. (1984), Informal talk given at the Arab Centre, St Antony's College, Oxford.

Magazines, Newspapers

Al Yom al Sabah, March, April, 1987
Al Wafd, Feb, March, April, 1987
Al Shaab, March, April, 1987
Al Ahali, March, April, 1987
Al Ahram, November 1986, March, April, 1987
Al Ahrar, March , 1987
Al Ahram al Iqtisadi, April, 1987
Middle East Times, Feb, March, April, 1987
Al Missawar, September 1983

3

POLITICAL CRISIS AND POLITICAL CONFLICT IN POST-1967 EGYPT

Hani Shukrallah

In observing political conflict in Egypt today, one is most struck by the fact that conscious and willful political action by all parties in the political struggle seems scarcely to affect the actual direction taken by political developments, including the fate of those political actors themselves. Political agency is always delimited by material conditions. The much greater prominence of the latter in Egypt during the last decade is, however, no mere assertion of a crude materialist perspective. For it is precisely when political agency is especially weak that political actors become more susceptible to the 'whims' of structure.

The most essential fact about post-1967 Egyptian society and polity is that the crisis of hegemony brought about by the June defeat, remains, two decades later, unresolved. Put very simply, this means that the growing weakness of the existing political system has not been transformed into the power of an alternative political force. A political conflict outside which the majority of the population remains, is one where the weak struggles against the weaker, while the less weak appears eminently powerful.

Methodological note

It is useful to begin this analysis by setting out very briefly, some of the basic theoretical tenets on which it stands. This is especially

53

important regarding state theory. It has for more than a decade been the focus of a wide ranging debate, which must inform any attempted theoretical analysis of concrete political reality.

The state is first of all a special material repository of the mode of production at a particular stage of its development, whereby the relations of production are already inscribed into the institutional materiality of that state. This mirrors, or translates, the system of class exploitation in the economic sphere, into a language specific to it and inherent in the specific role historically assigned to it by the prevalent division of labour. Put simply, the state is *a priori* - i.e. before the classes or class representatives controlling the state enter into the analytical picture - *rigged* in the interest of the dominant mode of production, and hence in the interest of the class or classes dominant within that mode or formation. The rigging mechanisms, however, express the state's own specific nature and are not mere extensions of the mechanisms or laws governing the economic sphere. Be they of the most basic nature, 'special bodies of armed men', or of a much more complex kind, such as the modern legal code or the hierarchical structures of the bureaucracy, they embody and reproduce class dominance irrespective of which group of class representatives controls the state.

However, once one moves away from that essential nature of the state, it comes into the analysis as the concrete product or special condensation of class struggles, themselves set within and delimited once again by a particular stage of economic development (Poulantzas 1980). This is not to say that the state is in continuous flux, adjusting itself in accordance with the changing fortunes of class struggle. Such a view would indeed make political crisis impossible.

Class struggles culminate in moments when they bring about a qualitative re-adjustment of the class balance of forces, causing a rupture in the prevalent political system and transmitting these adjustments into the form of the state. The new state-form becomes structured in a way that does not merely crystallise or ossify the balance of class and political forces of which it is a synthesis, but operates in accordance with laws which are inherent in the new forms and which reproduce the general nature of that specific culmination of previous class struggles. The new form is, therefore, no mere passive product of a specific juncture in the class struggle, awaiting further developments to readjust accordingly. On the contrary, it is an active, vital force playing a determinant role in all future class struggles. Obviously, there are fairly small ruptures, expressed in minor or non-essential readjustments of the state form, and drastic ones that do away (essentially anyway) with one state form and replace it with another. However, the latter may indeed express some kind of compromise between the old and the new dominant political groups and hence retain some aspects of the previous state-form.

It should be stressed, however, that the areas in which class struggles express themselves in the state are already delimited by the inherent class nature of the state. Class struggles can and do determine the ways in which class domination is expressed and exercised in and through the state. They cannot, however, change the fact of that class domination unless they change the fact of the state itself.

The above should help shed some light on a persistent problem that has beset the theoretical analysis of post-1952 Egyptian society and polity. The problem is perhaps common to the analysis of the Third World, rather than simply to Egypt, although Egypt provides a notable case in point. It lies in what may be called the dogma of development. Development in this sense is perceived as an over-riding 'obsession', furiously driving the economy or mode of production, classes and class interests, elites and elite goals, as well as the state itself. The state, in turn, goes on to define everything anew, again in accordance with the requisites of development. From this perspective, development becomes the defining principle of every aspect of the social formation. It gives them all a circular kind of coherence, whereby the explanatory validity of the goal of development on one end of the analysis is 'proven' by locating it on the other end.

Consequently, into a specific type of state is collapsed a whole edifice of already determined international local, historical, economic, social, institutional elements. Another edifice of pre-determined needs, requirements and functions which are relevant to explaining the origins of the state as themselves pre-determined expressions of the other two, is added on top of those. Politics and economy, state and class, etc., have no separate existence, but are all lumped together according to an inexorable and inherent logic of development, which subordinates everything in the Third World to its essential plan. Real history disappears in front of an abstract schema of modern Third World history: national and class struggles, be they massive, violent, or small, have nothing conjunctural in them, but serve only to point development in the direction set by the all powerful requirements of development.

Unlike the debate on the modern Western state which has tended to emphasise its uniqueness and specificity, the debate on the 'Third World' state has continuously tended to lump together as many levels of the social formation as possible. In this way it seeks to arrive at one *raison d'être* or essential logic that explains it in its totality, as well as in the minutest aspect of its detailed existence. With the Western state, whichever way it is made to relate to other elements of the social formation, and whichever way it is situated within a structure of causality and determination, the trend of the discussion has been away from its simple reduction to this or that determinant element or organising principle outside it. Given the concerns which this raises and the areas it illuminates, such an approach would appear to be of considerably greater utility in the analysis of the Egyptian state.

The June 1967 defeat and the evolution of the crisis of hegemony

The resounding military defeat of 1967 threw the Nasserist regime, state, and society into severe crisis. A structural crisis of the Egyptian capitalist economyhad already been in the making. The war in Yemen and the intensifying struggle between the regime's military and civilian wings had the markings of a political crisis of sorts. Most significant was the fact that the majority of the bourgeoisie, massively restructured as a bureaucratic bourgeoisie a few years earlier, was already beginning to think about moderation: a halt to attacks on the private sector, a freer hand in running the public sector and in dealing with the private sector, and freer access to the world capitalist market.

The economic crisis

The defeat did not merely 'develop' these elements of crisis, it appropriated and redefined them within a qualitatively new historical conjuncture, the basis of which lay in a rapidly maturing general crisis of hegemony. While this study will concern itself with the particular condensation of this general crisis in the political sphere, some of the complexities of understanding the determinate role of the economy should be dealt with here.

The economic crisis hides three levels of contradictions. The first of these levels is the most profound, setting as it does the deepest material basis for the whole crisis. It is the level at which economic conditions determine the general laws governing the social formation. The crises arising out of military defeat and the pressure of continued military occupation, were the dynamic elements that in a very short span caused the capitalist mode of production to exhaust its 'progressive' capacities. Indeed this 'historic shift' has a general Third World aspect which has been treated by many authors, who have argued about the decline of the 'national bourgeoisie' of the Third World.

The historically 'reactionary' phase of capitalism does not correspond in this analysis, either to non-development or to non-industrial development. A general way in which the end of the progressive role of the bourgeoisie can be determined, is to determine whether it has, for all practical purposes, completed the achievement of the domination of capitalist relations of production in the social formation. However in the concrete, historical terms of Egyptian capitalism this process could be summarised very briefly as follows: a) capitalism in Egypt could no longer develop in antagonism to Western imperialism and relatively independently of it, but had to do so in co-operation with it; b) capitalist development could no longer be tied to the expansion of state control over the means of production, there should be a division of its communal ownership amongst its individuals and groups; c) the dominant bourgeoisie could no longer ally itself (however precariously) on the international level with the socialist, progressive countries and movements; d) on the Arab level, it was no longer a force supporting the forces fighting imperialism and traditional classes in the area, but was increasingly allying itself to them; e) ideologically it ceased to expound ideas and cultural products of a humanist and rational character and gave more and more prominence to ideological elements that are obscurantist and anti-humanistic.

The second level on which the making of the crisis in the economic sphere could be discerned, is that constituted by the historic crisis of 'Egypt's particular path of capitalist development'. Specifically, it is the structural crisis of the relatively independent, import-substitution model of capitalist development. The contradictions generated by development based on this stratety, were rapidly leading it to a dead end. The one-sided expansion of the manufacturing industry - although created in a necessary climate of protectionism and antagonism *viz-à-viz* the world capitalist market - was suffering from intense pressures pushing it towards a qualitative restructuring of its links with that world market. Modern, industry-based, capitalist relations of production had in Egyptian conditions, to be tied to a concerted attack on the links which integrated and subordinated the country's agricultural pre-, semi-, and backward capitalist structures to the world market. However, as agriculture was largely freed both from the dominance of its most backward structures and from dependency on the world capitalist market which those structures provided, it became in the process subordinated to industry-centred, modern capitalist relations of production. Industry started to generate strong pressures for deeper dependency links with the world capitalist market. The new 'dependency' was to be based on modern capitalist relations of production, rather than on backward relations of production and was to become centred on the dominance of the modern 'national' bourgeoisie as opposed to the commodity producing landed aristocracy.

Obviously the above two levels are intimately related. The structural crisis of relatively independent import substitution capitalist development, contributes to the historic 'exhaustion' of the 'progressivity' of the capitalist mode of production, on the economic level, as well as to provide one of the most important mechanisms that bring about this historic transformation. The distinction between the two levels is, however, very important, particularly in view of the distortions which the dogma of 'development' has brought to the analysis of the current crisis in Egypt. The first level concerns the historic 'maturity' of capitalism in Egypt, indicating the loss to the exceptional 'primary' and 'revolutionary' period of its life. The second signifies that a particular type of capitalism has become moribund, and cannot survive for much longer. It does not signify however, that capitalism is incapable of transition to another mode of existence.

The third distinctive level concerns the specifically economic results of the defeat of June 1967 and the resulting occupation of Egyptian territories. The enormous burdens which the war and the rebuilding of the armed forces put on an economy that was already in crisis cannot be overestimated. Not only did industrial expansion practically come to a standstill, but even the maintenance of the existing structure of industry was becoming increasingly more difficult. Again it is important to make the distinction between the effects this particular condition had on the more profound contradictions in the economy in society, and its more superficial forms. The economic results of the defeat (combined with its results on all other levels of the social formation) constituted the basic condition within which all the contradictions of the social formation were qualitatively reconstituted. This did not mean, however, that these results were irrevocably tied to the more profound processes they helped set in motion.

In conclusion, the defeat helped affect a historic transition of capitalism in Egypt, bringing about once and for all the end of the 'progressive' side of its existence. The related structural contradictions of the relatively independent, import substitution mode of existence of Egyptian capitalism were brought by the defeat to a situation of intense crisis. This crisis - which remains with us to this day - can by resolved either by a complete rupture with the capitalist mode of production and the transition to socialism, or by the success of that capitalist mode of production in transforming itself into a new mode of existence. Since the inauguration of 'Infitah', the Egyptian economy has been in a process of transition towards that new mode of existence. The more obvious effects of the defeat on the economic level were in fact substantially relieved through the peace settlement, the 'open door' policy and the multi-faceted effects of the 'oil decade', all of which were loosely connected and occurred in the second half of the 1970s. They helped reduce the intensity of the structural crisis, postponing its 'moment of decision' and giving more 'breathing space' to the transition period.

The political crisis

In July 1952, the take-over of state power through a military coup overthrew the dominant alliance of the landed aristocracy, the Monarchy and British colonialism, but did not hand it over to the 'national bourgeoisie' in their stead. Coming from within the transitional state itself, the conditions of class struggle which drove the 'Free Officers' to make their coup allowed them to retain power for themselves and to 'disenfranchise' all of civil society. Not only did they not hand state power over to the bourgeoisie, they denied it that share of power it was able to attain under the Monarchy. The 'Free Officers' denied all classes and class factions any access to state power and established the supremacy of the state itself over civil society. It was not, however, a classless state, but (precisely) a bourgeois state, since the whole state is inscribed with a class nature that is embodied institutionally and ideologically on every level of its structure. Capitalism was already deeply imprinted on the transitional state, which had to rid itself of its decadent upper crust formed by the Monarchy, a thin layer of aristocratic bureacracy, and forms of British penetration (that had already been substantially weakened, first in 1919 and then in 1936) for it to be transformed into a purely capitalist state.

The new masters of this state were loath to let go of the power they had seized, faced as they were with a bourgeoisie that was so frightened of the developing popular movement that it had all but totally withdrawn its support from its classical political representatives, the Wafd party. The latter was so torn between the growing radicalism of its mass popular base and the growing conservatism of its middle class base, that it became increasingly incapable of moving either forward or backward. The popular classes for their part were increasingly frustrated and dissatisfied with their national leadership in the Wafd, but were still incapable of going forward on their own.

The 'Free Officers', on the other hand, were trained in an ideological school that responded to the questions posed by the contradictions of capitalist development and class struggle in a discourse that was radical as much as it was anti-democratic. It was an ideological school that grew out of the acute crisis of authority that beset Egyptian society at the time, and was especially suited to their position within the apparatus of the state. Standing at the top of the state, which had become supreme, they were freed from the constraints of direct ties with the bourgeoisie on the one hand and the dangers of the popular movement on the other. Faced at the same time with the weakness of the political will of civil society, whose combined political force confronted the young officers most ineffectually in March 1954, they forged ahead building their own dominion, setting up the absolutist supremacy of the executive, headed by an all powerful President and leader of the nation.

The new state-form could be seen as a special form of Bonapartism. It was based on the maintenance of the subordination of civil society to the state. The development of Egyptian Bonapartism in conditions of a revolutionary transformation of society from above, as well as in conditions of intense and violent confrontation with western imperialism, caused by the exceptional threat of the state of Israel, helped shape the peculiar laws of Egyptian Bonapartism.

The most distinctive feature of the state-form of Nasserism, was the degree of success it was able to achieve in de-politicising, de-mobilising and de-organising the Egyptian population. It is, indeed, difficult to find a similar example anywhere else in the Third World. Whether we look as far as Peron's Argentina, or as near as Ba'athist Syria or Iraq, so-called 'populist-authoritarian' regimes depend on some kind of organised social and political base. Nasserism did not suffer from the absence or weakness of such an organised base. On the contrary, its absence was an essential law of its political system and a sign of the exceptional level of success it was able to achieve.

The Nasserist state-form was built on the systematic destruction of all forms of political and social organisation of the popular classes on the one hand, and their direct relationship with the 'leader of the nation', on the other. Nasserism was able to achieve an outstanding level of political and ideological hegemony among the mass of the popular classes. Its anti-imperialist stance, the victories and successes it was able to realise in its confrontation with imperialist West, the attacks it made on the landed aristocracy and later on big private capital, the great industrialisation drive and the associated construction of an enlarged working class, all formed the basis for a feeling of 'identity of interest' between the wider popular classes and the regime. However, the systematic destruction of all the existing forms of mass organisation combined with the above mentioned successes to create the specific discourse of Nasserist despotism. In this it is the leader of the people who has the sole responsibility for identifying and anticipating the peoples' interests and wishes and for taking the initiative to realise them, in the form of gifts handed down from above.

The political organisations of Nasserism (The Liberation Rally, The National Union, and finally The Arab Socialist Union) were essentially organisations of state functionaries. They were charged with giving legitimacy (through their mere existence) to the liquidation and prohibition of other political organisations. At the same time, they helped reproduce the 'individualisation' and 'de-organisation' of the masses by embodying these processes in their institutional structures. This was reproduced in every other form of mass organisation such as trade unions and professional associations.

The individualised and de-organised popular classes served, however, as the cudgel held by the all-powerful President to enforce the subservience and obedience of the mass of the bourgeoisie, and to discipline the ruling elite. The double-edged law of Egyptian Bonapartism was that the regime's ideological and political hegemony over the popular masses had to be sufficiently strong to allow them to be the President's tool against the economically dominant class, while denying them any independent initiative. They were to be maintained as a passive tool, to be wielded by the president only as and when he himself saw fit.

The decline of Egyptian Bonapartism

The defeat of June 1967 was a massive blow to the foundation on which the state-form of Nasserism was erected. However, the historical transition of the dominant bourgeoisie from a progressive to a reactionary class goes beyond the form it took as expressed in the ideological and political defeat of Nasserism. A whole tradition of culture, values, world outlook and political principles had since the beginning of the century given the country what current Egyptian intellectuals (for example: Mohammed Hassanein Hikal and Tarik al-Bishry) have termed, 'Al-Gamee Al-Qawmi', which might be loosely translated as 'the national unifier'. The assumption behind this is that since the rise of the modern national movement, the great majority of Egyptians have been to a large extent united by a sense of common identity and interest. This 'unifying' national discourse was provided by the Egyptian bourgeoisie and expressed its ideological hegemony. It reflected the objective basis for this hegemony in the form of a 'material' area of identity of interests between the various 'national' classes, illustrated by the 'renaissance' and the creation of a modern secular national identity, by the struggle against the colonialists and the landed aristocracy, and by economic and social progress. The transition of the Egyptian bourgeoisie into a reactionary class has removed the objective basis on which its ideological hegemony hitherto leaned. It has given rise to the kind of ideological crisis that has beset Egyptian intellectuals for more than a decade, causing them to lament the collapse of unifying national values and nostalgically hearkening to a golden age gone forever.

Thus, while the wider and more subtle elements of national ideological hegemony passed into crisis, it was natural that the more directly partisan and doctrinaire ideological hegemony of the political regime of Nasserism should suffer an even harder fate. The resounding crash of Nasserist ideological hegemony, was the vital mechanism of the intensification of that wider ideological crisis of the class as a whole. A great many essential tenets of Nasserist ideology came tumbling down with the military defeat of 1967. The principal ideological justification for despotism was 'national unity' against the external enemy. Inherent in the position of the all-powerful leader was his ability to 'wrest victories' for his people on their behalf, and in a way that precluded their attempting to get victories for themselves.

The weakening of the ideological hegemony of the Nasserist regime was expressed immediately in the intensifying crisis of its political control. On the famous 9th and 10th of June 1967 Nasser was restored to his position of enormous power through the initiative of the popular masses. While inherent in the discourse of the Egyptian Presidency is the responsibility of the President to the people in the abstract (through his ability to embody their will and to anticipate their needs and desires) he is responsible to no one in concrete terms. On the 9th and 10th of June 1967, the people for the first time actively and of their own initiative chose the President. The message was not lost on those concerned; if the people can keep the great leader himself in power, so too they can have a say in how he exercises it.

With the weakening of the regime's ideological and political hegemony over the popular classes, its grip on the bourgeoisie also weakened. This highlights one of the laws of motion governing the post-1967 transformation of the Bonapartist state-form in Egypt. It predates Sadat, and in fact set the trend which Sadat was later to elaborate in his own way. This was the tendency of the state-form to respond to its growing crisis of political control over the masses by giving concessions to the bourgeoisie. This was the basic content given to the promises and ideas of 'contained liberalisation', that came as a response to the political crisis resulting from the defeat. The testimony of several leaders of the time states that Nasser had contemplated and discussed the possibility of forming an opposition platform within the Arab Socialist Union, and that he offered the leadership of this platform to the right wing of the 'revolutionary command council', represented by Baghdad and Kamal Hussein. This is very revealing of the subtle beginnings of the processes of transformation that were to become much more pronounced in later years.

Firstly, there is the direction of the concession. Although Nasser was being kept in power and retained his control of the bourgeoisie, the state and the ruling elite through popular support, he did not seriously contemplate ways of organising this popular support. On the contrary, he thought of passing minor concessions to the bourgeoisie, the majority of whom stood to his right. Secondly, not only was the concession restricted to a minor consultative capacity, but also this capacity was to be handled by political representatives assigned by the regime to talk on behalf of the bourgeoisie. It did not extend to allowing it the right to choose for itself even this minor voice.

This tendency was scarely developed in Nasser's time, however. Nasser retained his popular legimitacy which he wielded against the bourgeoisie and the ruling groups around him. It was Nasser's death, the succession of Sadat to the Presidency and the ensuing power struggle, that gave a great push to the development of the political crisis and to the transformation of the state-form and political system.

The popular classes could no longer provide the President with any basis for his supreme power. In fact they were beginning actively to challenge the continued suppression of political and civil initiative and organisation. This was clear even before Nasser's death, in the wide scale student and worker demonstrations of 1968.

To assert the power inherent in his position against the other members of the elite, Sadat did not appeal to the popular masses but to the mass of the bourgeoisie. Responding to their desire for a share in political power, and in order to reassure them against the apparently whimsical twists and turns associated with Nasserist times, his slogans of the 15th of May 1971 were 'the state of institutions' and 'the sovereignty of law'. These were meant to imply that the time of revolutionary upheavals was over, that private property would henceforth regain its sanctity, and that the bourgeoisie would be able to have more access to the state machinery and more say in policy matters.

Paradoxically, in weakening the Nasserist state-form, Sadat bolstered its most central constituent element, the power of the President. Nasser depended on his appeal to the popular masses to use as a cudgel against both the bourgeoisie and the 'core elite' at the top of the state. Sadat depended on the mass of the bourgeoisie (both inside the state - the 'bureaucratic bourgeoisie' and in the private sector), who were beset by two profound feelings. The first was a deep gratitude to the President who was breaking down the barriers to their claim to the great accumulated capital of the state, and who was restoring the sanctity of private property. Furthermore, he was bringing Egypt back to its natural allies in the capitalist West, and in resolving the national crisis caused by the Israeli occupation, defusing a time bomb threatening to blow the whole capitalist system apart.

The second profound feeling holding the mass of the bourgeoisie in its grip was fear. It was the fear of a class beset by a severe crisis and unused to government. It had been wholly reconstructed and massively enlarged through the most ruthless aggression on private property, making private property especially susceptible to renewed aggression. It had had to face severe conflict with its natural allies in the capitalist world, while holding to an uneasy alliance with its natural enemies in the socialist camp. The leadership of a heroic despot such as Nasser, although providing the conditions for its massive expansion, had kept it in continuous fear for its future existence and subject to his apparent whims, to his radicalism and to his 'adoring' base of the popular classes. Finally, there was the fear brought about by the rising leftist reaction to the national crisis.

Nasserism's seemingly whimsical twists and turns and its appeals to popular classes were, in the end, part of a system of control. The masses could be brought out for massive demonstrations, but were immediately returned to whence they came, while the supremacy of the state apparatus, encompassing as it does the supremacy of the bourgeoisie, remained unchallenged. The great chasm separating those who were 'beih's' and those who were not, is unchallenged and its reproduction assured. The demonstrations of the students and workers, the national committees which Sadat claimed were emulating the 'Soviets' of the Russian revolution, the appeals to Vietnam's struggle and the demand that arms be given to the independently organised students, workers and peasants - all this presented the bourgeoisie with what it believed was the real and serious threat of communism. This was not the 'communism' that it used to accuse the Nasserist regime of, but something totally different, unfamiliar and incomprehensible. The 'communism' of Nasser was after all designed and implemented by other 'beihs', and however radical sounding, they were familiar people who belonged to the same sporting clubs and enjoyed a similar style of living.

Thus, while the students and workers' movements were striking against the despotic structures of the state-form and demanding rights and freedoms at the base of the political system, the state-form was attempting to transform itself from above. Sadat's 'democratic experiment' of the three platforms inside the ASU in 1975, was the first sizeable step taken in the attempt to adapt the despotic state to new conditions generated by the crisis of hegemony. The concessions were two-fold: firstly, wider participation from the bourgeoisie, as expressed in the 'right wing' platform, secondly, an attempt to contain the mass movement of the left, by giving concessions to those sectors of the leftist political intellegentsia that had until recently been in a form of alliance with the regime.

The development of the crisis, however, was such as to make the attempts at adaptation themselves a new element in its intensification. The limited, if ineffective political expression allowed to the political intellegentsia which had been historically tied to the regime, but shed from its institutions in the context of 'liberalisation', no longer provided a safety valve. Most of all, the depth of the crisis was expressed in Sadat's determined drive to the right. In the age of the advance of the bourgeoisie, the special freedoms enjoyed by the President had allowed Nasser to be extremely sensitive to the possibilities of advance. This had enabled him to put himself on the far left of the bourgeois intellegentsia. In the age of retreat, this same position made Sadat especially sensitive to the dangers of procrastination. He, therefore, forged ahead to bring about what he believed was an inevitable end, convinced that the price of the delay might very well be his regime itself.

The drive to the right, the anger of the mass of the petit-bourgeois and the bourgeoisie intelligentsia, Sadat's policy on the national question and the growing mass movement making riots and strikes an almost daily occurrence - all combined to intensify the political crisis, and to widen the scope of the concessions beyond the original intentions of the regime. The platforms which were allowed to become parties had not been in existence for one year before the bread riots of January 1977 erupted and made their previous existence unbearable to the regime. The flaw in the process of adaptation became apparent: concessions directed at fairly 'safe' sectors of the intelligentsia which were intended to help contain the anger of the popular instruments, added more fuel to the flames. The growing mass movement made use of the least effectual of opposition criticism to whip up a higher level of struggle. At the same time, the whiff of those struggles, coupled with Sadat's peace drive, acted to increase the appetite for political power among the most mild natured of bourgeois political representatives and heightened their own anger at the President and his clique.

Two basic elements of the political crisis

To make theoretical sense of the political crisis, its evolution and the ways in which political conflict takes shape within it, it will be helpful at this stage of the discussion to look at the development of its two basic constitutive elements in relative separation from one another. These are what we may term 'the crisis from above' and 'the crisis from below'. Their development is by no means synchronic. It is therefore necessary to elaborate the distinctive characteristics and laws of motion of each, and the ways in which they are combined and articulated within the development of particular struggles.

1. 'The crisis from below'

This is provided at its most basic level by the historical transition in the nature of the relationship between the national bourgeoisie - which has given ideological and political direction to the 'people' for close to a century - and the rest of that 'people'. Prior to 1967 the popular classes were joined to the great mass of the bourgeoisie (and under Nasserism) with the bourgeois state and regime by a sense of 'national unity' and common national interest, which excluded only a 'tiny minority' of 'imperialist lackeys'. Class identity was never totally subsumed by this but subordinated to it. After 1967, however, it entered a new stage of rapidly intensifying crisis and disintegration. Popular discontent, mass resistance, a sense of class division and class hate, were all not merely severely intensified, but reconstructed in a qualitatively different way.

The crisis 'from below' was quite rapid in developing. The workers and urban poor who came out in support of Nasser in the immediate aftermath of the defeat on the 9th and 10th of June 1967, very soon came out against the Nasserist regime (though not quite against Nasser himself) in February and then in September of 1968. With Nasser's death and Sadat's accession to power, it developed rapidly. The power struggle between Sadat and the 'Nasserist' clique, further weakened the regime's organs of political control (which had been in the hands of the 'Nasserists'), as well as the overall status of the regime. Three strands of popular protest developed dramatically: the student movement, the workers strike movement and the phenomenal development of riots among the urban poor, euphemistically termed by the regime 'regretful incidents'.

The full significance of the 'crisis from below' for the maturity of the crisis on all levels, could be revealed through two examples expressed in the testimony of two men who at various times were closely associated with Sadat. The first is provided by Mussa Sabri (former chief editor of the government daily *Al-Akhbar*) in a book documenting the October War. The book includes minutes of meetings between Sadat and his chiefs of staff, at which he sought to convince them of the necessity for the large military operation that was to be the October War. One of the foremost arguments used by the late President to counter the resistance of the chiefs of staff to the idea of war was to point out the extreme dangers posed by the mass movement, especially the student movement. Clearly, the student movement on its own could not hope to threaten the regime, and Sadat was neither so naive nor so 'weak-kneed' (if anything he was quite the opposite) to believe that it would. The danger of the student movement arose from the general atmosphere surrounding it amongst the popular classes. They were by no means ready to seize power but were quite capable of preventing the regime from enforcing genuine and profound changes upon the state-form.

The second example is provided in the testimony of Hassan Al-Tohamy, who was a close aide of Sadat and whom Sadat made much use of in preparing the ground for his visit to Jerusalem. According to Al-Tohami, it was the massive uprising of 18th and 19th January 1977 that decided Sadat on the visit to Jerusalem. These uprisings, which included millions of workers and urban poor, convinced Sadat that if he did not reach an immediate settlement with Israel, the future of his regime was open to question.

A most important aspect of the 'popular movement', distinguishing it clearly from the *pays legal* of the intelligentsia-bound, organised political opposition, was that it forged its own tools of action. The civil rights it seized as means of expression, organisation and protest, were overwhelmingly de facto rights. They were protected in the short term by the level of movement in particular sectors and at particular times. However, they were subject to relapse as soon as that level fell, or as intense confrontation with the state brought about severe repression. The 'national committees' of the students, the 'committees of workers deputies' in some factories, wall newspapers and posters, leaflets, rallies, occupations, demonstrations, strikes, and so on were all products of mass action created by that action itself, capable for periods of time of achieving a precarious de facto stability (this was especially true of the years of the student movement in the first half of the 1970s). It was a stability, however, continuously contested by the regime's repressive apparatus, which incurred arrests, detentions, deployment of anti-riot troops, expulsions and administrative punishments of various kinds. Especially worthy of mention here is the use, at a certain stage, of the civil 'Islamist' groups. This was decisive in destroying the defacto democracy that the student movement was able to enforce in the universities in the first half of the 1970s.

It should be made clear that the defacto rights seized from below are not without connection with de jure transformations from above, the lion's share of which goes to the 'privileged' sections of society. Directly and indirectly, benefits did find their way down to lower levels of society. Sadat's 'corrective revolution' of 1971, whose 'liberalisation' was so openly directed and limited to the bourgeoisie, nevertheless provided indirect benefits which were immediately made use of by sections of the popular classes below.

To defeat his opponents at the top of the state, Sadat had to attack the already much weakened 'Arab Socialist Union' and the official but clandestine 'Vanguard Organisation' within it. Neither was in any way a serious instrument for organising the masses in support of Nasserism. This was revealed in May 1971, when the masses watched passively and indeed with a fair amount of glee as Sadat struck his triumphant blow against the 'Nasserist' clique, which seemed to have control of the great bulk of the state apparatus, as well as of the 'ASU' and of its secret vanguard. The latter, while extremely ineffective organs of organisation and mobilisation, were much more effective as organs of control and repression. Their connection with the security apparatus was openly symbolised by being headed by the Minister of the Interior himself. The destruction of the 'Vanguard Organisation', and the virtual death blow to the ASU as a whole, created a vacuum of political control from below, which various sections of the popular movement were quick to exploit. This was not merely a matter of weakening the capacity of the state for direct repression, because, on an even more profound level, it directed further blows at the whole edifice of ideological hegemony based on the traditions of bourgeois nationalism.

Another extremely important benefit the popular movement derived from institutional changes from above, was the restoration of a level of respectability and power to the 'judicial' organ of the State. This was an extremely significant adaptation of the state-form. In order to bolster the power of the President against the rest of the ruling elite, and to decide the power struggle at the top of the state in accordance with the desires and the mood of the mass of the bourgeoisie inside and outside the state, the bourgeoisie had to be given some access to state power, as well as a reassurance that the 'age of revolution' had given way to an age of stability, institutions and legality. Directed at the bourgeoisie, and limited by the retention of the absolute supremacy of the executive, as well as by a legal code that practically denies all civil and political rights, it nevertheless gave the de facto 'liberties' - which the mass movement was able to seize at different times - a certain institutional protection against the more extreme forms of repression by the executive.

A third more obvious benefit was that provided by allowing political concessions and rights to the bourgeois intelligentsia and to the 'elite' of the petit-bourgeois. The establishment of legal opposition political parties, the relaxation of restrictions over freedom of expression and the establishment of an opposition press, all provided the popular movement with an immensely expanded battery of anti-regime propaganda, with information about itself and aided it in its defence against state repression. It did not, however, provide it with a path towards political evolution and organisation.

It is one of the basic features of the peculiar development of the crisis from below, that the popular classes remained essentially outside the arena of political struggle. Acting most profoundly on the development of the crisis as a whole, they remained singularly incapable of translating the results of their actions into political gains for themselves. A number of elements combined to produce this result, the most important of which will be dealt with here.

First of all, the heritage of Nasserism left the popular classes exceptionally poorly equipped, both politically and organisationally. As pointed out above, the mass organisations of Nasserism did not work to mobilise the masses behind the regime, but rather to reproduce the liquidation of all forms of mass organisation. Popular mobilisation was a function of a direct relationship between the 'leader' and his 'people', with which the regime's own mass organisations had little to do. These at best acted as government bureaus charged with dealing with individual grievances, and at worst mere extensions of the multitude of police and intelligence organs. The degree of success this achieved can still be seen in the dominant discourse of workers' trade unions, which a decade and a half after the end of Nasserism remain essentially constructed as a specialised kind of government bureau, rather than as an instrument belonging to the workers movement.

It should also be stressed that under the above conditions, the popular classes underwent a dramatic transformation in their make-up. The industrialisation drive virtually recreated the working class, with the majority of the reconstructed class having never known the political and trade union traditions which that class had accumulated in the pre-1952 era. The re-emergent popular movement had to contend with this extreme level of de-organisation before it could hope to transform itself into an effective political force.

None of the reconstructed elements of the new political movement legal or illegal, on the other hand, could justifiably claim to express a political continuity enjoying some kind of popular political base, however limited. Again, the exceptional success of Nasserism, unexplained by the mere fact of despotism, is revealed in the extreme isolation of the political intelligentsia from the popular classes, the majority of the former being appropriated into the regime's political organisations, with the remaining few consigned to their homes or to the regime's prisons.

In the post-1967 era, it was essentially in the student movement that a certain level of integration between a limited political intelligentsia and a relatively wide mass movement was achieved; in the first half of the 1970s by the left, in the second by the Islamists.

The new, leftist student activists who led the student movement of the early 1970s, constituted what was for all practical purposes, a new section of the Egyptian political intelligentsia. Having little or no contacts with the older leftist tradition in the country (the latter basically appropriated by Nasserism), they were a product of the post-1967 era, of the defeat of Nasserism. As such, they saw themselves as an alternative both to Nasserism and to that earlier leftist tradition itself.

As a section of the popular mass movement, the student movement occupied a special place. While not being itself an integral section of the 'intelligentsia' strictly defined, it occupied nevertheless an intermediate place. Without going into the various ideological, social and other structural elements that characterise the student movement , suffice to say it provided no direct access to the popular movement outside the universities. The process of its politicisation (both in terms of easy access to political struggle and in the nature of the forms of that access) functioned in accordance with laws quite distinct from those applicable to other sections of the popular movement.

Another highly significant feature of the student movement should be mentioned here in passing, as it provided a popular base for the political intelligentsia, and was at the same time its most important source of new recruits. This feature was to have quite distinctive effects on political developments in the country. The student movement was not merely a source of new blood that would provide the political arena and specific political movements within it, with dynamic and youthful activists, but for the left and the Islamist movement it was to be the source of what continued to be - at least relatively - distinct sections of both.

Thus, while the new wave of leftist political action was successful in forging and leading a large scale popular political movement amongst students, the links it created with the popular class, and particularly with the working class, remained too small. Operating within the inherited political and organisational conditions, it was too weak to bring them rapidly into the arena of political struggle. These links were not without effect, however. Being largely confined to the industrial working class, unlike the new cadres of the Islamist movement, the left was never successful in creating important links with the urban petty bourgeoisie, those links played a significant part in developing workers' economic struggles. Indeed, the most important workers' strikes from 1971 onwards placed a largely new generation of leftist workers at their head. This was especially true of the more organisationally developed examples, such as the 'committees of workers deputies'.

The process of the defeat of the leftist-led student movement and the growing prominence of Islamist influence within the universities began as early as the end of the October War. It was not, however, before the events of January 1977, that leftist influence was almost totally eradicated from the universities, which were almost totally inherited by Islamist forces. In defusing the most intense expressions of the 'national question', the October War took the wind out of the student movement's sails. It had an almost opposite effect on the movement of workers and urban poor, however. Freed from the ideological 'blackmail' of the necessity of a 'solid internal front' against the foreign enemy, the development of the strike movement and the rise in the spontaneous resistance of the urban poor, was on a scale unprecedented since the anti-British national movement on the eve of the 1952 military take-over.

A new element that played a highly significant part in limiting the influence of the left in the working class movement, common also to the left's defeat in the universities, was constituted by a most effective ideological development. The ideological elements of what may be called 'national defeatism', which had been advancing since the moment of the June defeat, achieved great prominence in the aftermath of the October War. The argument that confrontation with the West and Israel had proven futile, that Egypt could not hope to face the 'Furious American Bull' as Heikal put it, that this confrontation had caused the country enormous hardships, resulting in a continous series of defeats, had been supreme amongst the mass of the Egyptian bourgeoisie practically on the morn of the June defeat. The first reaction of the popular classes, both immediately after the defeat on the 9th and 10th of June, not only insisted on resistance, but strengthened Nasser's hand sufficiently to be able to check the demands of the bulk of the bourgeoisie for several years. This reaction was sustained through the 1968 student and workers movement and was evident at Nasser's funeral, when the national leader was bid goodbye by millions of Egyptians chanting 'We shall fight'. The student uprisings of 1972 and 1973 were possibly the highest expression of this will to resistance. This will was, however, always articulated in various ways and to different extents with its opposite. In the minds of the popular classes the national confrontation had for a long time been coupled to despotism and economic deprivation. After 1967 it became further coupled with defeat, in a way that connected it in a single chain to 1948 and to 1956 (which for the first time was discovered to have contained a military defeat). The October War was such that it almost overnight restored the influence of 'national defeatism' amongst the popular classes. The successes it achieved were sufficiently impressive to defuse the feelings of national humiliation, and its limits and scope were so constructed as to confirm in the most powerful terms the 'futility' of continued confrontation. Sadat's first message to the people, even as the war was still going on, was 'America has entered the war against us, I cannot fight America'. Unlike his 'fog' speech of 1971, the message strongly hit home.

As pointed out above, the post October War conditions put a further check on the spread of leftist political influence in the popular movement, while paradoxically giving its economic resistance tremendous impetus, thus recreating the conditions for leftist linkages and influence amongst its ranks. It was in the aftermath of the uprising of the 18th and 19th of January 1977, however, that the slightly earlier developments, ushering in what has come to be called 'the oil decade', made their effects felt on Egyptian society. The pinnacle of the popular struggles that preceded it, the uprising of millions of workers and urban poor, was at the same time the sign of its collapse. This spontaneous uprising brought the full weight of the repressive state apparatus upon the popular classes on a previously unimaginable scale. Unable to control the rioting by its large anti-riot squads, the state brought in the army and hundreds were killed and wounded with hundreds more arrested, and new laws, giving sentences of life imprisonment for participation in strikes or demonstrations were introduced and publicised in the headlines of the national press.

The lull that would normally be expected to follow a confrontation of this scale, acted only to dramatise the effect of the processes brought about by the 'oil decade'. January 1977 can be seen as the point at which the crisis from below underwent a radical turn. It helped turn what would have been a more gradual decline, into a collapse. The great wave of migration to the oil rich states, both in Libya and the Gulf, brought much social upheaval to the popular classes. The multiplier effects of the migration wave have been discussed in detail elsewhere. Suffice it to say that on a 'man-power' basis (including the total male and female population between 6 and 65 years of age), put by the 1976 national census at above 25 million, more than 2.5 million migrants were estimated to be living outside the country during most of that decade.

Amongst the popular classes no one seemed to remain in the same place long enough to sustain the sense of solidarity and common interest that is a condition for mass struggle. Those who did migrate (ironically the most dynamic worker-activists were at the same time among the most capable of finding avenues for migration) almost invariably transformed themselves into petty investors of one kind or another. Those who did not, found a great many avenues for more than doubling their incomes either through moving to the new sectors opened up by the economic boom and the 'Infitah', or by taking on more than one job. At the same time, a great number of avenues were opened by the boom and its accompanying inflation, which enabled many to move out of the class of wage earners altogether. The working class was in a continuous state of flux, with workers leaving (either to migrate or to another economic sector) to be replaced by newer and less experienced workers. Another important development, that had a dramatic effect on the workers' movement (especially in the public sector, which employs the overwhelming majority of the modern working class), was the fact that employers accepted the possibility of workers holding down more than one job and used this to bring real wages down to below the subsistence wage. A second job became a necessary condition of survival and was responsible for more than half of many workers' incomes. The struggles over a few pounds of incentive or bonus became of much less importance in relation to their real income than they had been in previous years.

Essential to an understanding of the peculiar evolution of the crisis from below, is the realisation that its 'unfolding' was, however, not restricted to its more relatively developed and overt expressions. As reiterated above, the most profound aspect of the crisis from below was the 'historic' crisis of bourgeois ideological and political hegemony. On this level, the crisis from below was continuously evolving, irrespective of the forms of expression of popular discontent. Though both obviously interacted and mutually reinforced one another, they evolved in accordance with distinct laws, the former undergoing a continuous evolution and intensification.

It is this that provides the key to undertstanding the peculiar development of the crisis from below in the late 1970s, when the continued intensification of popular discontent, of class hatred and of the most profound alienation from the state and the rulers, corresponded to an extremely dramatic decline in all forms of popular protest, organisation and action.

These were the conditions in which the Islamist movement, which had initially evolved in the universities in close co-operation with the police organs, became the strongest political focus available for the expression of popular discontent. It was one, however, that moved within the confines of dominant ideology, within which religious ideology was gaining an increasingly prominent space. It was subjected to a process of adaptation to, and appropriation of, elements of popular discontent, producing its own type of radicalism. In spite of its beginnings, as soon as it began to evolve into a political trend, whose sphere of action was defined by the ranks of a section of the popular movement, it came to embody and express in its own way, the intensifying anger of the popular classes. Indeed the intensity of the development of the crisis can itself be detected from the transformation of what at first appeared a mere creature of Sadatism, into the force that so dramatically ended his life in 1981.

It is important at this point to deal with the popular myth that has portrayed the Islamic student radicals as something qualitatively different from their leftist precursors, closer somehow to what is itself a mythical Islamic people. Both movements drew on almost exactly the same sections of the student population - essentially its poorer sections. The leftist base may have been slightly tilted towards students with urban origins, and the Islamists slightly more towards those of rural origins. In the first half of the 1970s, the left was no less a dominant political force in the universities of the rural towns than it was in those of the great urban centres in Cairo and Alexandria. The latter day bastion of *Jihad*, Assyut University in Upper Egypt, had at an earlier period been one of the most successful examples of the leftist-led student movement, claiming amongst its activists a few of the latter leaders of Jihad itself.

Ironically, the more successful the Islamists were in bringing about the defeat of the left in the universities, the more radical they themselves became, appropriating and reconstructing elements of the discourse and forms of struggle developed by the left. Both inside and outside the universities the radical Islamists were able to spread the network of their political influence much wider than the left was ever able to do. The argument being made here is that this level of success was first and foremost a product of a peculiar and original coupling of an increasingly intensifying crisis of hegemony with an extremely low level of popular struggle. A movement that arose within the domain and institutional instruments of dominant ideology, while at the same time acting as a vehicle for the expression of popular discontent, was most suited to those conditions.

Unlike the left, the radical Islamists outside the university found their political base, not in the ranks of the working class movement, but amongst the poor urban petit-bourgeois. There however, they created an incomparably wider base than that produced by the links the left had had with the working class movement. An important difference is worthy of note, nevertheless. For it was an essential characteristic of the Islamist movement that it never led or gave direction to the kind of mass protest that the left had known in the student and workers' movements and has been able to resume lately in the latter. The upper Egyptian cities of Assyut and Minia are notable exceptions, however, and indicate that where the radical Islamic movement is most powerful, it is both capable and motivated towards employing the tactics of mass protest. The fact remains, however, that a venture of this kind requires an immensely greater number of activists.

One further point needs to be made here. In spite of enjoying a much wider popular mass base than any other political movement, the radical Islamist movement cannot be said to have brought an effective section of the popular classes into the arena of political struggle. The terrorist tactics that are such an intrinsic and inescapable part of the make up of radical Islamism are both a cause and a result of this. It is first of all a natural outgrowth of an individualised but extremely intense class discontent. This objective basis, from which the movement derives its special strength, is constructed within a rigid political and ideological discourse, that is strongly confirmed by the traditions and specific experience of political Islam generally, and most especially by the militant tradition derived from Sayed Qutb. The latter is a product of a period of most extreme isolation for the Muslim Brotherhood, a fate it shared with every other political movement in the country.

The violent repression to which the movement is exposed as a result, works for its part to reproduce its relative isolation. The assassination of Sadat and the subsequent violent repression of radical Islamism, set the ground for a reconstitution of the Islamist movement in Egypt. It was to bring the moderate Muslim Brotherhood out of virtual oblivion and to reconstruct the movement under its leadership.

The oil decade has come to a dramatic end. Great waves of returning migrants, economic recession, the collapse of small businesses, the debt problem that has finally relieved the Egyptian government of what IMF officials have termed, its 'January 77' complex, rising unemployment on a scale not seen since the late 1950s, early 1960s - these are the new conditions within which the crisis from below is taking shape. The resumption of the workers' strike movement, opening as it does the door to a higher level of organisation of the working class, may develop at a sufficiently rapid pace for it to enter the arena of political struggle as an effective political force. The greater maturity of the crisis from above, on the other hand, opens the door to another radically different possibility. This is, to the utilisation of the confrontation between the state and the popular classes, in order to institute a change from above. In either case, as will be shown below, the new conditions can only bring the crisis of the state-form to a new and much more intense plane, one that leaves its future maintenance open to question.

2. The crisis 'from above'

On this level we are looking at the crisis as it is expressed and developed at the top of the state and society. It is important to note the way in which the 'Bonapartist' character grandiosely instilled into the Egyptian Presidency by Nasser himself, proved to have an especially potent capacity to utilise the most diverse of new elements of political struggle, in order to re-bolster and reproduce presidential supremacy over state and society. Standing at the heart of the state-form, the survival of this particular type of

Presidential supremacy reinforces and is reinforced in turn by the survival, in essence, of the state-form as a whole.

The two, however, do not march to exactly the same tune. There have been many examples where presidential supremacy was able to derive new sources of power from the weakening of the state-form as a whole, and even where the reproduction of presidential supremacy *required* the further weakening of the state-form as a whole. The foremost example of the latter was the case of Sadat and his 'corrective revolution'. There is an abundance of examples, on the other hand, where the President played no part in directly weakening the state-form but has been unable to resist the temptation of making use of that growing weakness in order to bolster his own power. Mubarak's presidency, for example, could not but make use of the self-same circumstance that gave him his inheritance - the grave fright which the assassination gave the whole ruling elite and the bourgeoisie - to set up a new supreme presidency. This has neither the legitimacy of the 'July revolution', the 'May revolution', or the October War, nor does the bourgeoisie; owe him anything for the historic road opened up by Sadat.

Holding as he does the institutional keys to the whole state-structure, the President is able to pit the various sections of the 'state-managers' one against the other. He is also able to make use of the mass of the bourgeoisie against all state-managers, to make use of the threat of the mass movement of terrorism or of an 'Islamic revolution' against the bourgeois mass, to threaten the organised political opposition with the military, and to keep the military at bay by making use of the 'hopes' that the opposition has put in him.

It is an inescapable conclusion nevertheless, that presidential supremacy is continuously being reproduced at a lower rung of a downward spiral. This is not a matter of degree of power but of the nature of power itself. Nasser set the popular classes against the bourgeoisie and the ruling elite; Sadat utilised the deep gratitude of the mass of the bourgeoisie; but Mubarak, enjoying neither the enthusiastic support of the popular classes nor of the bourgeoisie, is reduced to a juggling act whose space is continuously narrowing and which expresses itself above all as a strategy of doing as little as possible. It is ironic, but highly indicative, that the Bonapartism that required the heroic courage of Nasser to be created and the adventurist daring of Sadat to be reconstituted in conditions of crisis and transformation, now owes its survival to the extreme caution that is the most distinctive feature of Mubarak's Presidency.

The weakening in the nature of presidential supremacy is reflected in the overall hierarchical order, the internal discipline and the cohesiveness of the state structure as a whole. The weakening of these latter elements, in turn, reacts to reconstitute a weaker Presidency. A most significant feature of this is the way in which the 'centres of power' at the top of the state have been reconstituted in the post 1967 era, in a manner that expresses the crisis of the state-form and intensifies it at the same time.

Centres of power are inherent to the despotic state of 'July 1952'. Ever since Sadat, however, their terms of reference have undergone a qualitiative transformation. Under Nasser the 'centres of power' referred essentially to themselves; to their hold over various parts of the state apparatus. The logic according to which the balance of forces between them could be determined, was indigenous to the state structure and to its various roles: repressive, political and economic. This was a time when the state as a whole stood in a position of supremacy to the economically dominant bourgeoisie.

The changing nature of the 'centres of power' reveals the way this relationship is transformed. Under Sadat, the centres of power became conglomerations that extended beyond the borders of the state structure. They were still based on the control exercised over sections of the state apparatus, but the state-managers wielding power over those sections were no longer drawing their power from their positions within the networks of power indigenous to the state. Rather, they became focal points of whole associations that combined sections of the bourgeoisie inside the state with sections outside it, with non-Egyptian economic, political, military or intelligence networks. The integrity and the independence of the state became violated at the highest levels of state-power.

This subversion of the integrity of the state is distinct from the process by which the bourgeoisie achieves more or substantial political control over the state. The latter process would require access to state power not merely by sections of the bourgeoisie, but essentially by the political representatives of this class. This is not the exercise of political freedom within the class, but the corruption of the state through the direct access to it of various bourgeois groupings, which could - and in fact does - correspond to the political disenfranchisement of the class as a whole. This process has fallen short of subverting the state-form, and of transforming it into the fairly wide-spread forms of 'oligarchic' bourgeois dictatorships that do not express the supremacy of the state over the bourgeoisie but the dictatorial control of the state by one section of the bourgeoisie over the rest of the class and all other classes.

Such a transformation would mean the essential dismantling of the 'July 1952' state-form and could not have occurred gradually. A much more radical political rupture is required for such a transition to occur. *It is above all the institution of the presidency that safeguards the essential supremacy of the Egyptian state.* The institution of the presidency, as it is structured in Egypt, enjoys an intrinsic integrity, and independence that is inviolate except by its effective dismantling. Even Sadat, who was party to various 'combines', domestic and foreign, and in whose interest he used his office, was, as President, subject to laws and determinates which dwarfed this aspect of his behaviour.

The crisis and strategic transition provided many forms of access for the mass of the bourgeoisie to the state. This was not just a function of the political crisis, but expressed a highly original process where the restructuring of the capitalist mode of production and the bourgeoisie was occurring under conditions of political crisis - and the crisis of a particular state-form that had itself given capitalist development a peculiar character. The process of re-integration and reconstruction of the bourgeoisie from the ranks of the bureaucratic and private sector sections of the class, involved massive linkages between the state and the private sector. The former came to provide the overwhelming source of capital accumulation in the economy, as well as the overwhelming mass of the re-constructed bourgeoisie. The latter has been intensely involved in a process of re-claiming privately the capital accumulation it was able to realise collectively.

One of the more important institutional forms of bourgeois access to the apparatus of the state has been through the limited expansion under Sadat of the powers allocated to local government. For if the higher echelons of central government had become subject to various forms of Egyptian and foreign infiltration, it was on the level of local government (from Governors down to village councils) that the boundaries between state and civil society became extremely vague, and the difference between the state power and the economic power of the bourgeoisie greatly narrowed.

It is interesting and perhaps ironic that parliament, which is supposed to be the principal instrument of bourgeois political rule, remained as it is to this day, a rather ineffective but vitally necessary instrument of legitimating executive and above all presidential despotism. The crisis of the state-form always stood well short of changing this essential nature of parliament, as expressed in its constitutional and legal position. It is guaranteed by the overwhelming domination of Parliament by the political party of the state itself, The National Democratic Party. This is the party of bureaucrats and state functionaries, whose dominance does not express the dominance of a particular political trend of the bourgeoisie, but rather the supremacy of the state over the whole of the bourgeoisie. The basis of its position is the political balance of forces between the state and the bourgeoisie. Unlike the balance of forces between different bourgeois trends this does not depend on the relative influence of any particular trend within the ranks of the class, particularly within its most powerful, economically dominant sections, but rather it depends on the reproduction of the state's repression and disenfranchisement of the bourgeoisie.

The crisis of the state-form was expressed in Parliament in a variety of ways which are worthy of a separate study. Two of these will be noted here. Firstly, as in the case of local government, Parliament provided the mass of the bourgeoisie, rather than its political representatives, with freer access to the state. It did this by performing two basic functions. It provided a forum for the expression of minor sectional bourgeois economic interests. The bourgeois members of Parliament neither legislate, nor even genuinely approve legislation, which is the absolute prerogative of the executive and finally of the president. Instead, they lobby the executive for certain non-essential policies, which are for the most part already approved by the executive 'elite' but which the latter is hesitating to implement (e.g. the proposed tenancy law in the interest of bourgeois landowners). A less obvious, though not less important function is the provision by Parliament of a place where various groups of 'bureaucratic' and 'private' bourgeois can meet, and wheel and deal to their hearts' content.

The second element is provided by the original discourse of Parliament. Whatever its real role, the Egyptian Parliament does occupy that part of the political system where the bourgeoisie can realise its political domination. Parliament's legitimating role must obviously draw on that original discourse. This gains in prominence as the crisis makes the overall legitimacy of executive supremacy more and more dependent on making concessions - minor though they are. The fact that Parliament does occupy this space, however, makes it an area where real concessions are extremely dangerous to the perpetuation of the whole state-form, while making it at the same time a focus of attempts to encroach on that state-form. This creates a highly contradictory situation where Parliament is one of the most resistant institutions to any genuine adjustments, while those adjustments that occur outside it can only intensify the pressures exerted on it. The politically organised intelligentsia can only look to Parliament for a way to realise its ambitions for a share in political power, putting pressure on Parliament to change. This makes its lack of change more flagrant and stark. The more the crisis intensifies and the more ambitious, confident and effective is the political opposition, the more pressure will be exerted on Parliament, finally eroding Parliament's legitimating role and transforming it into a focus of crises.

Another highly significant aspect of the 'crisis from above', was that provided by what we might call 'the rebellion of the judiciary'. It should be stressed at the outset, however, that the 'judiciary' within the Egyptian political system should be treated as being in an intermediate location between the state, on the one hand, and the bourgeois intelligentsia, on the other. It is the organ of state which is most accessible to the bourgeois intelligentsia, since it is highly responsive to its moods and sentiments. One of the first concessions made by Sadat to reassure the bourgeoisie about the end of the age of 'revolutionary legitimacy' and the establishment of the stable 'rule of law', was to restore to the judiciary some aspects of its inviolability and respect. The historical humiliation of the Egyptian judiciary at the hands of the executive of the July 1952 state, the ideological discourse inherent in the judiciary as an institution of a particular type which tends to defend civil and political liberties against the encroachments of executive power, the rising atmosphere of discontent and anger within the bulk of the intelligentsia, of which the judiciary is a prominent section, the self-pride also inherent in its peculiar institutional discourse - all are elements and contradictions which appear to have accumulated in a certain way within a certain conjuncture, to produce this phenomenon.

What the phenomenon entails is the unwillingness evinced repeatedly by the judiciary to implement a large part of the battery of repressive laws in existence (many of which could lead to sentences of up to life imprisonment for such diverse forms of political activity as strikes or marches, belonging to an illegal political organisation, etc.). On the contrary, wherever possible, the judiciary in Egypt has offered explanations of the established law that would help tie the hands of the executive power. Sadat was forced by this phenomenon to search continuously for new and tighter laws, which for the most part again the judiciary ignored.

This process has come to create another deeply contradictory situation, whereby the executive is forced to resort to the use of exceptional legal powers such as emergency laws and military courts etc. It cannot once again usurp the new-found judicial powers without striking at the whole basis of a political system that has become adjusted to the new realities of class struggle. A complete about turn of this kind would be a serious threat to the existence of the political system as such. This is an inherently contradictory situation. The usurpation of judicial powers intensifies the judicial rebellion, and vice versa, while the more the crisis intensifies in other areas, the more the state will need a compliant judiciary to use against its opponents. The judiciary however, will be more responsive to the mood of those opponents themselves.

A final essential element of the maturity of the 'crisis from above' is of course that provided by the politicisation of the bourgeoisie as a class. It has been stressed above that the political crisis was expressed essentially in the increasing cleavages between the bourgeois intelligentsia, on the one hand, and the state on the other, and in the cleavages inside the state itself. The bourgeoisie did not make use of the increasing weakness of the state to try and seize political control over state power, or even to transform the balance of forces between it and the executive to such an extent as to break the latter's exclusive monopoly over state power.

A number of essential elements accumulated in such a way as to reproduce the political apathy of the bourgeoisie and its servility to the state. The most important of these lies in the fact that the bulk of the class - and more significantly, that fraction of it exercising control over the key sectors of the economy - was formed within the state, and was in fact the product of the state transforming itself into a dominant class faction. As is clear from the above however, there is a distinction between the despotic supremacy of the state over the rest of society and the dominance in the economic sphere of the bureaucratic bourgeoisie. The logic of the exceptional predominance of a bureaucratic bourgeois class fraction was such that it was created politically servile, with real political power held exclusively by the topmost summit of the class, corresponding to the highest echelons of the state apparatus. The fact that the mass of the bureaucratic bourgeoisie was as politically disenfranchised and powerless as the private bourgeoisie can be clearly seen in the development of class and political struggle in the country.

The massively expanded bureaucratic and private fractions of the class entering into a process of re-integration in the post-1967 era, nevertheless formed a class that as a whole has had very little experience of political power, one that is more used to being ruled than ruling. It is a class that has been badgered and subjected to a discipline enforced from above for so long, that it finds it very difficult to conceive of itself as exercising political mastery over the society which it dominates economically.

It is, furthermore, a class that is economically dependent on the state. This massive edifice of accumulated capital remained the major basis for the extraction of surplus value, combining both private and bureaucratic capital and being exercised through plunder and through the de facto and/or de jure privatisation of the state economic sector. A study of the concrete data of Infitah would show that it was in fact this that has hitherto formed the most substantive content of the policy of Infitah, while reconstruction of ties of economic dependency with the world capitalist market remain relatively undeveloped. This latter conclusion, it might be mentioned in passing, goes against the prevalent dogma about Infitah, which has reduced it to the relatively insignificant expansion of imports of manufactured goods. The economic dependency of the class on the state, however, does not necessarily correspond to its total political subservience. It acts as a support for this only when articulated with a whole set of other conditions brought about by the development of class struggle and the specific heritage that is the product of previous outcomes of class struggle.

Inherent in economic dominance, nevertheless, is the desire for political domination. If, under certain conditions of class struggle, this desire is checked, other conditions may help intensify it. The crisis which produced intense opposition within the bourgeois intelligentsia under Sadat, produced at the same time the most enthusiastic support among the ranks of the mass of the bourgeoisie for Sadatist despotism. It was, in fact, fascinating to see how little support was enjoyed in bourgeois ranks by the immense conglomeration of bourgeois politicians, trends and parties including the Wafd, the old 'rightist' wing of the 'Revolutionary Command Council', the Muslim Brotherhood, and notable personalities like Heikal and the Amin brothers, to whom we can add the continuous influx of former ministers and politicians of various sorts, who went to join the ranks of the opposition. With the assassination of Sadat things began to change on this front too.

The rise of Islamic ideology

Nationalist, relatively secular ideology had exercised a preponderant hegemony, at least since the revolution of 1919. It became supreme after 1952, when it also took on a 'socialist' tinge. With the defeat of 1967 it went into a crisis so sharp it was more akin to collapse.

This set of ideological elements, which are termed nationalist/secular as short hand, does not encompass all of dominant ideology, which is a much wider and a much more complex phenomenon. The latter not only includes a wide range of reconstructed, inherited, ideological elements, it also takes on a wide variety of forms, as it is coloured by the position and experience of the different classes and class fractions in the society, each giving it a tint of its own. The hegemony of 'nationalist' ideology meant that it provided the organising principle around which the whole range of elements that combine to form dominant ideology were constructed and derived their coherence. Its crisis is inevitably, therefore, a crisis of dominant ideology as a whole.

To view the rise of Islamic discourse as an expansion and a reconstitution of an already present element of dominant ideology, in the context of its intense crisis, is important. It frees the analysis of Islamic fundamentalism from the prevalent dichotomy that has made it either a bourgeois conspiracy, whose architects range from Sadat to Saudi capital, allied to the so-called 'parasitical bourgeoisie', or a popular reaction to westernisation and the Infitah. Furthermore, it rejects the view of Islamic ideology as some sort of eternally inherent and essential state of being of so-called 'Islamic societies', submerged for a while under the imposed westernisation of colonialism and 'westernising elites', but intrinsic to some abstract Islamic people who remained untouched by this westernisation.

On the contrary, the full complexity of ideological production must be brought into the analysis. Delimited by the conditions of a bourgeois society that has lost all its previous vigour, and stimulated by a crisis of hegemony of dramatic severity, the most diverse elements - professional ideologists and laymen alike - are most powerfully driven to reassess the conditions of their existence. So long as they do this with 'bourgeois eyes', that is, within the confines of dominant ideology, they can but draw on that bag of conceptual tools supplied by that dominant ideology itself.

Islamic ideology was amongst the more prominent 'responses' from within dominant ideology itself to its crisis, set within the context of a wider general crisis of hegemony and the post 1967 'historic transition' of bourgeois society to a conservative stage of its existence. It must be emphasised here, however, that i) it was not the sole ideological response, and ii) the expansion it came to know was by no means automatic, nor inevitable. Neither the forms, nor the levels of hegemony it realised were already inscribed - in embryo - either within it, or within those general conditions. For each new expanded and redefined space it carves out for itself within dominant ideology, Islamic ideology would have to go through a process of de-articulation, reconstitution and rearticulation, a process that does not occur in a vacuum, but is rather itself continuously subjected to the effects of class struggle and concrete developments. These do not operate on it as outside factors, but rather as elements of that process itself.

It would indeed be difficult to see in the 'Islam' of the veil and the beard of the late 1970s the mere 'growth' of the elements of Islamic discourse articulated within the dominant ideology of pre-1967 times. To explain this it is necessary to examine some of the effects of the upheaval of the oil decade and the related massive wave of Egyptian labour migration to the oil states.

1) The most dramatic of these was the original co-joining of intensely higher levels of class antagonism on the one hand, and the

drastic decline in all forms of popular resistance and movement on the other. This took place within the context of a predominant persuasion among the popular classes towards the ideological element of the 'individual solution'. Here we have a very interesting example of the way an ideological element which is already inherent in the 'individualising' effect of capitalism on these classes, not only was itself qualitatively reconstituted and expanded by historical developments, but was capable both of operating separately, through a discourse of its own, and at the same time suitable - under specific conditions of class struggle - of being incorporated into another discourse, namely Islamic fundamentalist discourse. The latter begins - even in its most radical forms - like all religious discourses, from the premise of an 'individual solution': society's problems or solutions originate in the individual's faith and the moral values of its members. Two ideological elements with different histories and traditions are thus brought together, mutually incorporated into each other and mutually reinforcing each other, under conditions that dramatically expand and enhance them both.

2) An obvious effect of the migration by hundreds of thousands of Egyptians to the conservative Gulf states, is the absorption to a certain extent of the dominant values, traditions and cultural norms of these societies. This effect is further enhanced when the wealth of these societies not only makes them major importers of Egyptian labour, but of locally produced and especially customised Egyptian cultural products. The expanded production and re-production of 'Islamic' ideological products in Egypt is powerfully reinforced by the great demand of the wealthy Gulf market.

3) The ideology of the family and of the subordination of women provides another interesting example. This had - for obvious reasons - remained throughout more closely attached to religious discourse. In the post-1967 era, however, the social effects of the improvements in the position of women were making themselves felt on the family, providing a basis for development of the misogynist elements, already inherent in this ideology. On the other hand, both the defeat and the resultant 'historic transition' of the Egyptian national bourgeoisie, evoke the most intense feelings

of national and class humiliation amongst the popular classes. In dominant ideology the loss of dignity is most profoundly co-joined to the loss of a man's control over his womenfolk, thus providing another basis for the development of misogynist ideological elements. Migration gives both a substantial push. In coupling the intensification of national and class humiliation to the decline of resistance as a means of regaining dignity, it helps make women an easy target for this 'restoration' of dignity. On the other hand, the migration intensifies the upheaval inside the family as the men depart, leaving their womenfolk behind to enjoy more independence and control over the household. Misogyny becomes one of the most powerful elements of reconstituted and expanded Islamic ideology. The removal of the veil, women's work outside the home, women's independence and the related stigma of 'promiscuity', are all seen as a principal cause of the evils of current life, intimately related to the loss of 'manhood', i.e. of personal dignity. However, the position of women in society as interpreted by the new Islamic ideology, is itself qualitatively new. It is by no means a mere restoration of that position in an earlier age, nor indeed of something that has lain dormant within some mythical 'Islamic' people dominated by a 'westernising elite'. The new construction of that position does obviously draw on age-old ideological elements, but as an integrated and internally coherent structure of today, it simply never was.

What is most significant is the distinction between the rise in the influence of Islamic ideology in the whole of the society from top to bottom, on the one hand, and the political power of the 'Islamist' movement - radical or conservative - on the other. Ideologically, the bourgeoisie as a whole, and with it the rest of the society was, especially since the late 1970s, becoming more 'devout'. Religious discourse was spreading to a multitude of conceptions and attitudes.

The beginning of this ideological process, as pointed out above, predated the spread of the political power of the Islamic movement, which of course was to play a significant role in bolstering it. But so did the state even before them. Sadat became the 'faithful President', espousing the 'values of the village' and a society based on 'science and faith'. As early as 1971 the new 'permanent constitution ' amended the Article on Islamic Sharia, making it into '*the* principle source of legislation', rather than its previous formulation as, '*a* principal source of legislation'. The state and the media confronted the challenge of the left in the early 1970s with a continuous harangue against atheist communism. This confrontation also included the conscious conspiratorial utilisation of Islamic discourse and the creation and bolstering of Islamic groups under the tutelage of the state and its security apparatus. Scenes reminiscent of the Germany of the 1930s became prevalent in the universities; book burnings and 'commie bashings' were an almost daily occurence. What must be emphasised here is that these transformations of state-espoused ideology, appear at one and the same time as a response to a growing market, and as the producers of the prevalent taste to which they once again respond.

The point is that neither the state nor the 'Islamist' movement can claim complete or even substantial credit for the process of ideological 'Islamisation ' of the society. Nor can they point to that process as evidence of the size of their support. While it is not denied that the Islamist movement is the greatest political beneficiary and bolsterer of the process, one cannot escape the conclusion that the two are by no means the same thing. This is a point that cannot be over-emphasised, in the face of the prevalent fascination with 'Islamic revival' in the writings of many 'Islamic' and Western 'orientalist' scholars alike. It is a fascination that has tended to attribute every sign of this ideological expansion to the special 'brilliance' of the Islamist movement, or to the way it is purported to 'reflect' the original Islamic sentiments of the people. The other side of this, of course, is to see an Islamic fundamentalist 'under every bed', to exaggerate the power of political Islam so much that one wonders why they are so hesitant about seizing political power for themselves.

Thus, in the first half of the 1970s, the slow and gradual expansion of Islamic ideology corresponded to the political support given to Sadat by the bourgeoisie and the political challenge in some sections of the mass movement presented by the left. In the second half of the 1970s the bourgeoisie's support for Sadat was further enhanced, while the political resistance by radical Islam rose and gained in strength. Essentially, however, it remained confined to sections of the educated youth in the student movement, with some spread outside among the ranks of urban petty bourgeois youth, such as petty traders and skilled labourers. Meanwhile, the space occupied by Islamic discourse in dominant ideology was growing at an unprecedented rate. Most interesting at this stage was that political 'Islam' corresponded to a radical petty bourgeois construction of the Islamic elements of dominant ideology. However, the 'moderate' Islamic ideology that was spreading within the bourgeoisie and the society at large, did not correspond at all closely to a rise in the political influence of moderate and bourgeois political 'Islam', as represented by the Muslim Brotherhood - the latter enjoying relatively minor political backing in the society.

In spite of the expansion of Islamic ideology over the past few years, it cannot as yet be said to have achieved hegemony within dominant ideology. The latter remains in a state of severe crisis, enmeshed in a mass of antagonistic elements, while despondency, apathy, the absence of a common direction, and the mosaic culture that has made Egyptian society appear as many different societies gathered in a single space, continue to express in the most powerful terms the intensity of the ideological crisis.

Indeed, for 'Islamic' ideology to achieve hegemony in the ideological sphere, it must first of all achieve a political triumph of substantial proportions. This is true, of course, of any rising ideology in the modern world. However, despite the economic and social power it has come to enjoy, it must have control of the state, and of both its repressive and ideological machinery, before it can set itself up as supreme. The mere fact of the discord of ideological and political 'Islam', means that the former remains unable to achieve hegemony, and is incapable of incorporating and subordinating the other elements that would combine to create a dominant ideology comparable to its general world view. The opposite is not necessarily true, however. A political conquest of the state may be an unavoidable condition for Islamic ideology to achieve hegemony, but that political conquest may not, on the other hand, lead to that achievement. Iran may be one case, but Numeiry's Sudan and Zia Ul-Haq's Pakistan offer very different cases. The degree and levels of hegemony achieved are not merely - or for that matter principally - dependent on ideological processes, but rather on economic and political elements, and most significantly on the way these elements are appropriated and reconstructed by class struggle.

The political apathy of the bourgeoisie, revisited

It is only after the dramatic death of Sadat that one began to see some political in-roads being made into the mass of the Egyptian bourgeoisie. Until that time, the bourgeois intelligentsia : writers, lawyers, politicians, political parties and trends, had been crying in a bourgeois wilderness. Not that their cries did not help push the crisis along. They are, after all, an influential group, but their influence was never extended to creating a real political base of their own, either within the bourgeoisie or among the popular classes. Interestingly, the bulk of the bourgeois and petit bourgeois intelligentsia went into a relatively long honeymoon with Mubarak in his first years of office, while their opposition has never reached the levels of intensity it did under Sadat. The historic transition had been already achieved and stabilised, while the assassination of Sadat left behind both presidential absolutism and state supremacy, capable of reproducing themselves but much weakened. This, while giving the bourgeoisie more self confidence in its relationship to the state in expressing a further development of the crisis of hegemony, also created the conditions in which that class was forced to begin some serious thinking about more stable political alternatives. This was especially the case since the new President could neither rid himself of Sadat's heritage nor claim it for himself. He could neither completely placate the political opposition amongst the intelligentsia nor liquidate it. A situation evolved whereby the 'play it safe' strategy of Mubarak, coupled with the weakened stature of his presidency (expressed in the proliferation of centres of power at the highest levels of the state) created a growing atmosphere of uncertainty amongst the bourgeoisie. The absence of a clear political strategy by the state, once again connected despotism to the possibility of sharp and unpredictable twists and turns so familiar under Nasser. To exercise political power by itself through political representatives who would owe their positions at the top of the state to its support, begins to look a more lucrative prospect to increasing sections of that class.

Two major political alternatives were already in existence; the conserative liberalism of the Wafd, and the Islamic fundamentalism of the Muslim Brotherhood. Other bourgeois political parties and trends remained incapable of posing themselves as serious contenders for bourgeois political support. It was the ability of those two political movements to carve out a political base for themselves in bourgeois ranks, that initially, at least, moved them towards being reconstructed as relatively viable and effective forces of political opposition to state supremacy.

The Muslim Brotherhood was, however, to prove the more successful of the two. The edge revealed by the Brotherhood in the 1984 general elections (which they fought on the Wafdist ticket), soon became a massive gap in the general elections of 1986. A number of elements combined to make the Muslim Brotherhood into the most powerful force of political opposition in the country. It was only natural that as soon as wider sections of the bourgeoisie began thinking about political alternatives, many of them would lean towards this espouser of a political doctrine that more consistently reflected the growing influence of this ideology within their ranks. Also of vital significance is the fact that the little challenged popularity of this ideology amongst the popular classes can be drawn upon by the Brotherhood and translated into political support. At one and the same time, the moderation and pragmatism of the Muslim Brotherhood reassures the bourgeoisie that any political changes undertaken with the help of its agency will cause as little pain as possible, while its political discourse remains capable of expressing to some extent the class and national grievances of the popular classes. Within the prevalent conditions of class struggle, the Muslim Brotherhood could appropriate these grievances within concepts of 'crusadism', 'westernism', the absence of 'personal values' and 'Islamic justice and charity', while limiting their sphere of effectivity to such things as communalist anti-Coptic sentiments, the veil and the workings of charitable Islamic institutions.

Developments in the 1980s combined further to enhance the political power of the Muslim Brotherhood and to reinforce its influence amongst wider sections of the bourgeoisie. For it was in the aftermath of Sadat's assassination that the balance of forces within the Islamic movement began to shift from the radical sections of the movement, such as the *Jihad* to the 'moderate' Brotherhood. The violent repression to which the former were exposed in the wake of the assassination, and the subsequent development of political support for the Brotherhood amongst some sections of the bourgeoisie, enabled it to incorporate a great section of the radical 'Islamists' within the bounds of its political scope. This success provided it with an invaluable supply of youthful and active cadres as well as direct access to sections of the mass movement in which those cadres had already made some headway.

This reinforced its influence within the bourgeoisie; twofold, firstly, by reconstructing it as a more effective political force, and secondly, by proving it capable of containing the unwieldly radical section of the Islamic movement. Even those sections of the movement that remained outside the political domination of the Brotherhood, such as the Jihad, were reconstructed by the new balance of forces to play the role of a cat's paw for the Islamic Brotherhood. They intimidated its enemies, fomented communalist hatred through their attacks on Copts (which the Brotherhood turns into political capital, while keeping its hands clean at the same time) and finally gave it, through attracting violent repression by the state, the ability to cash in on the sympathy which that repression generates.

A rather incidental but immensely significant development also worked to enhance the political power of the Muslim Brotherhood. Not only was the Brotherhood extending its political base within the bourgeoisie for the reasons stated above, but it was able in addition to transplant a ready-made, but most powerful 'Islamic' bourgeois section, nurtured and grown in Saudi Arabia and the Gulf States.

For as historical accident would have it, the most early migrants to the Gulf were the political emigres of the Muslim Brotherhood. By virtue of the political and ideological services they could render to its rulers, both domestically and regionally, as well as by virtue of their technical abilities, they were able to become close advisers and confidants of the most powerful groups exercising political and economic control of the Gulf. The 'oil decade' made everybody in the region immensely richer, while the 'Muslim' emigres were also perfectly situated to mobilise Egyptian migrant earnings for investment and black market exchange. Soon they built themselves into what effectively are great banking concerns, while the 'open door' policy and political relaxation had brought them back as powerful sections currently operating in the Egyptian private sector, retaining moreover very strong economic and political contacts in the Gulf region.

The growing politicisation of sections of the bourgeoisie was to find expression within the state apparatus itself. As the crisis of hegemony intensified, and as the internal discipline and cohesiveness of the state apparatus declined, the bourgeoisie - as a class - had been gaining wider access to them on a multiplicity of levels, and this opened up certain venues for the political infiltration of the state. These political in-roads into the state apparatus remain rather limited, and the monopoly of real power in the hands of the President and an extremely small group, although weakened, remains intact, thus further limiting their sphere of effectiveness. This does not mean that this process may of itself lead to a gradual annexation of the state. Its real significance lies rather in the way it first of all adds a new element to the intensification of the crisis of hegemony inside the state, further subverting its internal discipline and cohesiveness. Secondly, it makes possible the neutralisation and even the utilisation of some of the less strategic sections within the state in the fight between it and its political opponents, thus enhancing the effectiveness of its external challenge.

Finally, it combines with all the other elements of the development of the crisis of hegemony discussed throughout this paper, to set a process going whereby a relatively strong contender for political power, enjoying a good political base within the bourgeoisie, may sufficiently infiltrate the state apparatus to be in a position to seize power. It would not have to wait until it had itself mobilised a substantial enough popular mass base to strike effective blows at the state as a whole from outside. Nor would it have to risk the confrontation that such a mobilisation would by necessity entail. Rather it can allow the dynamics of the crisis and the more effective blows delivered upon the state through the spontaneous agency of the popular masses (that will necessarily accompany such a development) to weaken the state to such an extent that it will practically fall into its hands. It is just such a possibility that the Muslim Brotherhood represents in Egypt today.

Bibliography

Abdalla, Ahmed, *The Student Movement and National Politics in Egypt,* Al-Saqi Books, London, 1985.

Abu al-Kheir, Abdel Rahman, *Zikraiati Maa Gamaat al-Muslimin: al-Takfir wal Hijra* (My memories with the Islamic gamaa: al-Takfir Wal Hijra), Dar al-Bouhouth al Ilmiya, Kuwait, 1980.

Bana, Gamal al-, *al-farida al-Gha'iba: Gihad al-Seif Am Gihad al-Agl* (The Hidden Imperative: the 'Jihad' of the sword, or the 'Jihad' of the mind), Dar Thabit, Cairo, 1984.

Bishry, Tariq al-, *al Haraka al-Syiasia fi Massr,* 1945-1952, (The Political Movement in Egypt, 1945-1952) Cairo, 1972.

Hamroush, Ahmed, *Kisat Thawrat Yuliu,* (The Story of the July Revolution), Vols. 1 & 11, Dar al-Mawqif al-Arabi, Cairo, n.a.

Hamroush, Ahmed, *Mugtamaa' Abdel Nasser,* (Abdel Nasser's Society), Dar al-Mawqif al-Arabi, Cairo, n.a.

Hinnebusch Jr., Raymond, *Egyptian Politics under Sadat: the Post-Populist Development of an Authoritarian-Modernising* State*, Cambridge University Press, Cambridge, 1985.

Hussein, Mahmoud, *Class Conflict in Egypt: 1945-1970*, Monthly Review Press, New York and London, 1973.

Kepel, Gilles, *The Prophet and the Pharaoh: Muslim Extremism in Egypt*, Al-Saqi Books, London 1984.

Poulantzas, Nicos, *State, Power, Socialism*, Verso, London, 1980.

Sayed Ahmed, Mohammed, *Mustaqbal Al-Nizam Al Hizbi fi Massr*, (The Future of the Party System in Egypt), Dar Al-Mustaqbal Al Araby, Cairo, 1984.

Waterbury, John, *The Egypt of Nasser and Sadat: The Political Economy of the Two Regimes*, Princeton University Press, Princeton, 1983.

Zakaria, Fouad, *al-Haqiqa Wal Wahm fi al-Haraka al-Islamia al-Mu'asira*, (Reality and Illusion in the Current Islamist Movement), Dar al-Fikr lil-Derasat wal-Nashr wal Tawzei, Cairo, 1986.

4

MIGRATION, INFLATION AND SOCIAL MOBILITY: A SOCIOLOGICAL INTERPRETATION OF EGYPT'S CURRENT ECONOMIC AND POLITICAL CRISIS

Galal A. Amin

'If, beginning with the eleventh century, we examine what has happened in France from one half-century to another, we shall not fail to perceive that at the end of each of these periods a two-fold revolution has taken place in the state of society. The noble has gone down the social ladder, and the commoner has gone up; the one descends as the other rises. Every half-century brings them nearer to each other, and they will soon meet. Nor is this peculiar to France. The various occurrences of national existence have everywhere been turned to the advantage of democracy: all men have aided it by their exertions, both those who have intentionally labored in its cause and those who have served it unwittingly; those who have fought for it and even those who have declared themselves its opponents have all been driven along in the same direction...' (Alexis de Tocqueville, *Democracy in America*, 1835).

Introduction

Even before the recent drastic fall in the price of oil, which in many ways affects the level of Egypt's earnings of foreign exchange, there was a strong and widespread feeling of a deep rooted 'crisis' in Egypt, permeating not only the economic but also the social, political and intellectual life of the country. Egyptian economists have, for a long time, complained of a number of economic imbalances and distortions: a chronic deficit in the balance of payments and a growing external debt, a chronic imbalance in the state budget, and an output and employment structure too heavily dominated by the service sectors. Saving and investment ratios have indeed reached unusually high levels over the last ten years but both depend on unreliable and insecure sources of foreign exchange: oil exports, remittances of Egyptians working abroad, the Suez Canal and tourism. Too much consumption, it is often said, is wasted on luxury imports and too much investment goes into 'unproductive' channels such as luxury housing and import trade.

Egyptian sociologists have a similar list of complaints. Corruption is widespread and there is a conspicuous lack of work discipline and disrespect for the law. Violence is increasing and previously unknown types of crime are spreading. Material values are establishing themselves, while productive and socially useful labour is losing in terms of social status and prestige. The quality of life in the city is rapidly deteriorating with increasing pollution, overcrowding, noise and ugliness, while the village is rapidly changing from being a producing unit into a consuming unit, and in both there is an increasing westernisation of social life accompanied by a growing respect for whatever is foreign and a disdain for everything national.

Political commentators, in their turn, complain of a weakening in the sense of loyalty and of belonging to the homeland, a preoccupation by all with the problems of everyday life, an absence of what is often called 'a commitment to a project of national revival and progress', the decline of interest in Arab Nationalism, and a growing political and economic dependence on the United

States. Finally, those concerned with intellectual life and national culture point to the spread of what is regarded as 'low culture': the growth of fanaticism in religious movements and their growing concern for ritualistic behaviour, the decline of the Arabic language as a means of expression in the mass media and the deterioration of the quality of education at all levels.

The most common way to explain all these manifestations of economic, social, political and intellectual crisis is to blame them on the economic and political reorientation of Egypt in the early 1970s towards what is known as Infitah or the open door policy.

This term is usually understood to mean three things: the opening of virtually all doors to the importation of foreign goods and capital, the removal of restrictions imposed on national investors, and the gradual withdrawal of the state from playing an active role in the economy. Many observers of the Egyptian scene find it easy to trace many of the problems listed above to this reorientation towards Infitah. The chronic deficit in the balance of payments can easily be attributed to the excessive leniency of the authorities towards the taxpayers, while the distorted economic structure can be traced to the abandonment by the state of its role as an active investor in agriculture and industry and as a regulator of private investment. So, many of the social, political and cultural problems can be said to be connected with the growing inequality in income distribution which in its turn can be attributed to Infitah.

While this explanation may touch upon part of the truth, one is inclined to think that it does not go to the heart of the matter. For whatever meaning may be attached to Infitah, it amounts essentially to a *negative* policy of removing restrictions and eradicating barriers, rather than forcing certain actions or initiating certain types of behaviour. Economic liberalisation simply *allows* consumers, investors, importers and exporters to behave in a certain way, but does not by itself *create* the motive or inclination to behave in this way. What I have in mind is something like the saying 'you can lead your horse to the river but you cannot force it to drink', and it is this desire to drink, or the lack of it, which I regard as the missing link between the policy of economic liberalisation and the various aspects of economic and social behaviour referred to above. To give one example of what I mean, economic liberalisation may indeed make the consumption or importation of certain goods possible, but it does not so easily make the consumption or importation of such goods desirable. The desirability or undesirability of such an act is more directly influenced by the levels of income of the potential consumers and their relative position on the social ladder. The same policy of economic liberalisation could not therefore be expected to produce the same results in two countries, say Egypt and China, with different social structures, levels of income and historical and psychological backgrounds. My main argument in this chapter is that many of the manifestations of an economic and social 'crisis' in Egypt could be more convincingly attributed to the change in Egypt's social structure and to a rapid rate of social mobility which has been proceeding at a very accelerated pace over the last thirty years, than to the mere change in economic policy in the 1970s towards Infitah. Economic liberalisation has indeed been one of the main factors accelerating the rate of social mobility, but it has by no means been the only factor. Important factors had been at work long before the 1970s, while other factors started in the 1970s, which may easily have occurred under a very different economic system. If this argument is correct, it would follow that it would be quite wrong to imagine that the mere reversal of the policy of economic liberalisation could by itself bring this 'crisis' to an end, but it would also be wrong to imagine that the current crisis could necessarily persist so long as economic liberalisation continues.

Before I embark on substantiating my argument, I would like to point out how little attention has been given to the economic and social impact of the rapid change in Egypt's social structure by economists and sociologists alike. One is inclined to think of this as an example of an important area of investigation being neglected, simply because it falls on the borderline between two disciplines - the economists leaving it to the sociologists and vice versa. The nearest that the economists come to a discussion of this issue is when they tackle the issue of income distribution, but even if the economists were to have comparable data on personal or functional income distribution over a period of time, which in the case of

Egypt does not exist, such data would hardly reveal anything of the changes that occurred in the social structure. The rise or fall in the share of say, the top five per cent or the bottom twenty per cent of the population would tell us nothing about whether the members of any particular group have risen or fallen in relative income or social status or on the changes that might have occurred in their sources of income. Similarly, the rise or fall in the share of wages, in contrast to income from property, would tell us nothing about whether some wage earners may have now become property owners or vise versa. Such figures on the changes in personal or functional distribution of income are 'dead' figures, those which are fitting to describe the changes in a chemical or physical phenomenon but not in a living organism like a society.

Sociological writings have unfortunately contributed very little to our understanding of the impact of social mobility on Egypt's current economic or social problems. Much has indeed been written on the changes in social values and in patterns of behaviour associated with economic liberalisation or labour migration, and frequent references are made to a deterioration in work ethics, the spread of materialistic values and the growth of political apathy. But hardly any attempt is made to show exactly how migration or economic liberalisation could be responsible for these changes. When social mobility is discussed, the concern is usually with providing some indicators of the degree of the change in social structure rather than with its possible relationships with other aspects of economic and social life. Thus, Saad El-Din Ibrahim's pioneering essay on 'Social Mobility and Income Distribution in Egypt' (Abdel-Khalek and Tignor, 1982) provides us with a wealth of statistics related to the rate of social mobility in Egypt between 1952 and 1979 and discusses some of its possible causes, but says virtually nothing on its impact. Moreover, considering the nature of available data and the lack of any standard for comparison, even the indicators provided leave us unable to judge whether the rate of social mobility has been 'high' or 'low'. To be told, for instance, that 34 per cent of Egypt's professionals in 1979 had their parents working in agriculture (Abdel-Khalek and Tignor 1982, p. 398), in the absence of any corresponding percentage for an earlier date or for another country, is somewhat like telling us that the temperature is 39 degrees without telling us whether it is measured along the Centigrade or the Fahrenheit scale.

What is perhaps particularly disappointing is the way Marxist writers in Egypt deal with the phenomenon of social mobility, since one would have expected them, more than anybody else, to be particularly concerned with the impact of class structure on the various aspects of political and social 'superstructure'. Egyptian Marxists seem, however, to be mainly concerned with the division of Egyptian society between the 'exploited' and exploiting classes, the 'productive' classes and the 'parasites'. The fact that important sections of the traditionally down-trodden classes may have improved in social status over the last few decades is quickly dismissed as unimportant in favour of emphasising that much of their new income originates abroad or in 'unproductive' activities, while the fact that some sections of the upper classes may have suffered a decline in their income and social status is glossed over with an emphasis on the fact that new 'exploiters' have taken their places.

Both types of emphasis may indeed be justified, but may also be no more interesting than the improvement that seems to have occurred in the level of living of many of the poor and the decline in the economic and social standing of many of the rich.

Factors behind rapid social mobility

We are all familiar with the variety of factors that contributed to the rise in the rate of social mobility in Egypt during the Nasserist era of the 1950s and 1960s, including the land reform laws of 1952 and 1961, the nationalisation and sequestration measures of the early 1960s, the raising of minimum wages and of the rates of income taxes, as well as the very rapid expansion of free education and other social services. To this one must also add the rapid increase in the rate of investment in agriculture and industry during 1957-65 which led to the absorption of large numbers of agricultural surplus labour in irrigation projects, particularly in the High Dam and in manufacturing and construction work in the cities. The sheer growth of the role of the army and government in the economic, social and political life of the country was itself a factor contributing to greater social mobility. From 1952 onwards, the military establishment had become a new and important channel of social advancement, while the growth of bureaucracy and of government-created political organisations provided new ladders for a great number of university graduates who could not be absorbed in agriculture or industry.

While several of these factors lost much of their strength in the 1970s with the gradual abandonment by the government of Nasser's 'socialist' policies, it is striking, and to some degree ironical, that the era of *laissez faire* of the 1970s seems to have witnessed a much higher rate of social mobility than that of the Nasserist era of 'Arab Socialism'. This could partly be explained by the fact that in spite of Sadat's weak commitment to the welfare state, no government during his reign could stand against the pressure of demand for rapid expansion in school and university enrolment. In fact, the expansion of university education was faster in the 1970s than it had been in the 1950s and 1960s, and probably went much further towards reaching the lower income groups of the population through the rapid expansion of university education in the provinces. Similarly, in spite of all the rhetoric of the 1970s claiming a commitment to peace and declaring the war of October 1973 to be 'the last war', the military establishment showed no sign of growing less rapidly either in sheer size or in acquiring privileges. Both education and the military establishment continued, therefore, during the 1970s, to function as channels for social advancement, but to these old channels the decade of the 1970s added some new channels of its own. One of these channels which gained much greater importance with the coming of the Infitah, was to be employed directly or indirectly in the service of foreigners. Such opportunities, which were extremely limited under Nasser's much more closed economy, came increasingly to be extended further down the social scale. Thus, apart from professionals working in foreign companies, banks and consultant officers, there were larger numbers of people from more humble social origins who joined the service of foreigners in the flourishing tourist services, import trade, real estate or by providing a variety of personal services. Apart from being able to realise higher incomes than would have been possible by working in an Egyptian institution, working in the service of foreigners could bring with them new symbols of social advancement, such as acquiring some knowledge of foreign language, the wearing of a uniform or merely carrying the name of an illustrious foreign firm. Two much more important factors, however, have contributed to the acceleration of the rate of social mobility during the 1970s: external migration and the rise in the rate of inflation.

Although the rate of external migration rose significantly towards the late 1960s, migration did not start to contribute significantly to social mobility until the mid-1970s. Before this date, most Egyptian migrants belonged to the relatively high income groups of the population and consisted mainly of professionals, administrators and high-level technicians. The structure of Egyptian migrants changed significantly, however, after 1974 when it started to be dominated by the unskilled and semi-skilled construction workers, craftsmen and agricultural labourers. In contrast to other channels of social mobility, labour migration and the unique feature of requiring very little education and hardly any capital since migration, now offered opportunities for social advancement to the virtually illiterate, and required no more capital than the price of an air ticket which could easily be borrowed and repaid out of the earnings of the first few months in the oil-rich country.

Another contributor to social mobility in the 1970s was the sudden acceleration of the rate of inflation, which ranged between 20 per cent and 30 per cent in the years following 1974 compared with no more than five to six per cent during the previous two decades. Many of the beneficiaries of inflation were certainly among the already better off, such as the big owners of agricultural land, the owners of urban property, who benefited from the soaring land prices and from the rents of furnished apartments, the owners of industrial and commercial enterprises, as well as contractors and the well-established, self-employed professionals. But there were also significant sections of the population who traditionally belonged to the lower income groups and benefited from inflation, such as the large number of craftsmen, construction workers and agricultural labourers who were not among the migrants but realised a big rise in their real income as a result of labour shortages created by migration. On the other hand, while inflation has certainly hit the small landholders, the old-age pensioners, the unemployed and the large number of lower level government employees and public sector workers, it has also lowered the real income of a significant section of the middle class consisting of government officials and professionals working in the public sector or among the new university graduates who failed to migrate or to find work in the newly established companies associated with the Infitah.

The impact of inflation on social mobility has not been confined, however, to its impact on the relative real income from the *existing* occupations of various social groups; no less important has been the change in the sources of income created by inflation. To appreciate the importance of this, one needs to think of the ex-army officer who left his job to work in an import-export office, the small government employee who started working as a taxi driver in his spare time, the absentee land-owner who started to cultivate his land for his own benefit, the craftsman turning into a small contractor and the owner of a modest urban property who discovered the possibility of renting his furnished flat to an Arab tourist, etc.

All these factors worked together during the last three decades to bring about a rate of social mobility which is probably greater than anything Egypt has ever experienced in its modern history, pushing up the social ladder large numbers of the population who traditionally belonged to the lowest levels of society and allowing them to compete successfully with sections of the middle class who have found their social status rapidly declining. It will now be argued that the resulting change in social structure explains much more of the current economic, social and intellectual scene than is usually recognised.

Social mobility and Egypt's economic crisis

Egyptian economists have, for a long time, been complaining of the high propensity towards lavish consumption associated with the open door policy of the 1970s. They have been pointing to a sudden wave of consumerism symbolised by the rapid increase in the consumption and importation of motor cars, colour TV and video sets, washing machines, air conditioners, American refrigerators and Japanese fans. The complaint is that this type of consumption is 'unnecessary', 'wasteful' and costly, in so far as it is at the expense of saving and investment and creates too heavy a burden on the balance of payments. There is also the complaint that much of what is privately invested goes into infrastructure projects for the benefit of high income urban dwellers. It may well be argued, however, that what may be regarded as 'wasteful' when looked at from the whole society's point of view, could be regarded as perfectly rational from the point of view of certain sections of the population who have just experienced a profound change in their social status. So, many of the goods and services that may be consumed or aspired to by the newly rising classes do not merely fulfil the simple function of satisfying certain consumption needs but serve a much more important social function as symbols of social advancement. Thus, to these newly rising classes, the private motor car is not simply a means of transport but mainly a status symbol declaring their ascendence to a high social class . Much of the increase in luxury imports and the resulting burden in the balance of payments can similarly be attributed not merely to an increase in income but to the increase in social mobility associated with it. Even the increase in the consumption and import of some basic foodstuffs can be explained in the same way, for a rise in the consumption of such necessities as rice, meat, and even wheat could serve the same social function for the lower income rural households as that served by consumer durables for the urban population.

Social mobility could also shed some light on the prevalent preference among the rising social classes for certain channels of investment. One obvious example is investment in residential buildings, where the replacement of mud-brick dwellings by red-brick housing is the main symbol of social advancement in the village, apart from the necessity for the new type of house to have access to electricity and to accommodate the newly acquired consumer durables. One could also add the investment of the returning rural migrant acquiring a taxi, minibus or truck, or the small commercial enterprise which caters to the new desires of the newly rising classes. This may also show how difficult it is for the government to resist the mounting pressure from the same classes for greater expenditure on public utilities in the rapidly expanding districts. More generally, one might expect the pattern of investment preferred by those social groups who have only recently had access to surplus income, would be quite different from that preferred by a more confident and more established social class. For the former groups, in contrast to the latter, investment in industry or agriculture may seem too risky, requiring more capital, a longer gestation period and greater experience than is required by investment in residential buildings, transportation, tourism or import trade. Much of what is regarded as 'unproductive' investment may therefore be largely the preferred types of investment by new types of investors with smaller amounts of capital, education and experience, a greater anxiety to prove their social advancement and less confidence in their ability to maintain their newly-acquired social status.

I find it important to emphasise the relationship between the new patterns of consumption and investment and the rise in the rate of social mobility for at least two reasons. Firstly, it should warn us against exaggerating the ease with which the restriction of certain types of consumption and investment could be enforced. Critics of the open-door policy often suggest the curtailment of the consumption and importation of such goods as motor cars, TV sets and other consumer durables, which may indeed be much easier to enforce had such consumption not been the result of such powerful motives and aspirations as those associated with the change in social structure. Thus, no degree of improvement in the public transportation system may be sufficient to dispense with the desire to acquire a private car when such an acquisition serves a purpose which is much more powerful than merely to be transported from one place to another. On the other hand, the same observation should make us somewhat less pessimistic about the possible continuation of the same patterns of consumption and investment into the distant future. If it is true that the emergence of these new patterns is largely the result of rapid social mobility, one may very well expect these patterns to give way to other more socially desirable patterns as the social structure becomes more stable. In other words, one may expect that as the present social turmoil starts to subside and as the rising classes gain greater confidence in their new social positions, less expenditure may be directed to lavish consumption and more investment expenditure may start to flow into more productive channels.

Acceleration of the rate of social mobility may also shed some light on the problem of the growing deficit in the state budget . Complaints about the tax system in Egypt usually refer less to the low level of tax rates than to the high rate of tax evasion. Tax evasion is, in its turn, blamed on the decline in moral standards and the weakening of loyalty to the state. But this very weakening of loyalty may indeed be seen as partly the result of the change in social structure and in the relative social position of tax payers, tax legislators and tax collectors. One may argue that there is a big difference between the attitude to the state of the old class of big landowners and industrialists who constituted the main tax payers in pre-1952 Egypt, and that of the new classes who made their fortune in the 1970s whether from migration, trade, real estate, land speculation or from being connected in one way or another with foreign sources of income. One would indeed expect the former classes to have a stronger sense of loyalty and to feel more indebted to the state - which provided them with the necessary infrastructure invested on their behalf in irrigation and drainage projects and which enforced the law and order necessary for the protection of their interests. In contrast, much of the new income and wealth accumulated in the 1970s may be attributed not to state activities but rather to its inactivity, to the merely passive role of the state in allowing people to migrate, and to its failure to regulate the rate of inflation and the pattern of investment. If readiness to pay one's taxes has any relationship to the sense of indebtedness of the state, the newly rising classes in Egypt would indeed be expected to show a much higher propensity to evade taxation than the older classes of taxpayers whose income came from agriculture and industry. The same weakening in the sense of loyalty to the state could also be expected from members of the legislative councils in the 1970s who increasingly came from this same class of *nouveaux riches* and who had no interest in patching up loopholes in the tax laws. It is also quite possible that the attitude towards the payment of taxes of someone whose taxable income is relatively recent, unreliable and irregular, and whose newly acquired income has served to raise him to a higher social class, would be very different from the attitude of another whose source of income is long established and more secure, whose social standing an increase in income or wealth would not basically change. While to the latter, the payment of taxes may be like dispensing with some extra fat of the body, to the former it may seem like giving away part of the flesh. But in periods of rapid social mobility, the propensity to evade taxes may be just as strong in the declining classes, who have every reason to resist an additional sacrifice that would only hasten their decline, especially as they see their new rivals - whom they regard as unworthy of their new wealth - unwilling to make a similar sacrifice. There belong to these declining classes a good proportion of tax collectors whose worsening social status makes them more amenable to the acceptance of gifts and bribes and whose self-confidence has been undermined by the increasing aggressiveness of the rising classes whose increasing defiance of the law seems to meet with the compliance and protection of the state itself.

I have already referred to the rise in the rate of inflation as one of the causes of the acceleration of the rate of social mobility, but it is also true that rapid social mobility may be one of the causes of greater inflation. For insofar as rapid social mobility raises the propensity to consume and strengthens the tendency to invest in those channels with a faster turnover of capital, it will result in raising the velocity of circulation of money which in its turn will tend to raise the rate of inflation.

Social mobility and the new patterns of behaviour

It is not difficult to trace many of the new patterns of social behaviour in Egypt to the rise in the rate of social mobility, so that much of what is commonly referred to as an increase in corruption, lack of discipline and the spread of consumerism and materialistic values could be little more than the reflection of an excessive inclination to capture new opportunities, to adapt to new circumstances or to avoid a rapid decline in social status. While the opening up of new opportunities for rapid social advancement whets the appetite of the newly rising classes, the threat of social decline weakens the resistance of the declining classes to all sorts of temptations. In these circumstances, to stick to one's principles and moral standards appears more and more as a luxury, while a new system of values attaches greater premium to flexibility, to the ability to exploit new opportunities and to develop connections with those who matter. Patterns of behaviour that were highly regarded in a more stable society are now less valued, such as sticking to one's word or promise, pride and personal integrity. Such values are less fit for a rapidly changing society where loyalty to old relationships, whether to a friend, wife, a place or a principle appears more and more as excessive sentimentality unbecoming to a person who is continuously rising or on the move. The increase in the rate of certain types of crime and the emergence of new ones may indeed be no more than excessive manifestations of the same tendencies. The collapse of newly-built apartment buildings, only a few months after their completion, the repeated encroachment on state-owned land, and the widespread use of bribes to government officials may only be the symptoms of an excessive panic of social decline on behalf of individuals who are only more impatient or defiant than the rest.

In periods of rapid social mobility, family ties tend also to weaken. Marriages may have taken place under circumstances which are no longer present, and new opportunities may now be available to the husband or the wife which did not exist before. Social mobility may also require a physical dislocation which threatens old ties, and an increase in the earning capacity of one of the two parties may create a new feeling of superiority which disturbs the old harmony.

It may also frequently happen that recent social mobility leads to the marriage of a couple who have achieved the same level of education and who have similar earning capacities but who have come from very different social origins which could ultimately bring out differences that were only thinly disguised. Children may also come across opportunities for material gain and social advancement which were not available to their parents, either because of superior education or through marriage, which threaten the traditional respect they used to feel towards their parents and may encourage them to dissociate themselves from their old environment. A father whose real income has been greatly reduced by inflation may also find it difficult to retain his traditional authority over his children and may lose self-confidence with a declining ability to meet their demands. On the other hand, a growing permissiveness in the treatment of children may emerge, with an excessive readiness to comply with their demands, however unjustifiable, on behalf of parents who are financially able to do so. For, in the case of newly-rising families, children may fulfil a function similar to that fulfilled by consumer goods, with an ability to display the newly-acquired wealth and to have access to new sources of pleasure which the parents may find hard to enjoy. Indeed, it is much harder for such parents to hide the traces of their poorer origins than it is for their children with their greater access to modern education , foreign languages and the newly-acquired consumption habits. For declining families, a similar tendency to show greater leniency towards their children is motivated by their anxiety to protect them from a decline from which they have just started to suffer.

In a book originally published in 1927, a prominent sociologist (Sorokin 1959, pp.565-8) presents an interesting thesis which may throw important light on a number of other changes in social behaviour which emerged in Egypt over the last two decades. According to Sorokin, in situations where the social structure is relatively stable, the lower classes tend to imitate those patterns of behaviour which are associated with the higher classes, but the opposite seems to occur in periods of rapid social mobility when the declining classes are inclined to adopt many of the values and behaviour patterns associated with the lower but rising social groups. There is very good reason to believe that this may be true. There is firstly the greater self-confidence acquired by the rising classes resulting from their economic success and allowing them a greater degree of self-assertion. Secondly, there is the sheer spread of their numbers, again resulting from their greater income, making their presence felt to an unprecedented extent in schools, universities, clubs and other public places which have for long been the protected privileges of the higher classes. Thirdly, there is the increasing infiltration by these rising classes of the media, acquired through their increased access to education and allowing them to spread their habits of thought and patterns of behaviour to the whole society. Exactly the opposite developments become the fate of the declining classes whose influence gradually recedes with the decline of their self-confidence *vis-à-vis* their new rivals and their gradual withdrawal from public life. Willingly or unwillingly, but often unconsciously, they come to accept and even adopt the new patterns of behaviour and even the moral values of the lower classes, and discard their own.

Thus, the age-old contempt for manual labour, which has always been associated with low income and low social status, gradually disappears with the success of an increasing number of manual labourers in raising their income and the level of education of their children, and with the increase in the number of young people who traditionally belonged to the higher classes but came to accept, under sheer economic necessity, performing manual labour. Eating and dressing habits, which have always been associated with rural or low-income urban dwellers, have begun to be adopted by higher income groups, together with a return to old-fashioned ways of furnishing the home, a new appreciation of traditional Arabic music and the discarding of the habit of giving western or Turkish names to children in favour of authentic Egyptian or old Arabic names which used to betray humble origins. The recent and amazing spread of the rural habit of embrace between men, even if they had just been parted, may be explained in the same way. But it may not be at all far fetched to see a connection between this tendency to adopt rural and lower-class values and the so-called resurgence of religious movements and 'Islamic revival'. For what is involved here is not a strengthening of religious belief as much as

the increasing observance of religious rituals and ceremonies, and
the stricter adherence to an outward pattern of behaviour associated
with Islam, such as the adoption of the veil by an increasing number
of women, the spreading of the custom of starting letters and
speeches by invoking 'the name of God, the Merciful and
Compassionate', the insistence of broadcasting the Friday prayers
through loudspeakers and the increasing tendency to interrupt the
day's work to observe the daily prayers on time. The fact that
current interpretations of Islam, which are widely accepted by
Egyptian university students and the new leaders of religious
groups in Egypt, are definitely less rational and far less
sophisticated than those prevailing in the early decades of this
century, has led some writers to complain of a general decline in
Egypt's cultural life. What seems to be closer to the truth is that a
major change has occurred in the social structure, so that leaders of
the Islamic movement no longer belong to a narrow circle of a
highly-educated elite, speaking to a small number of urban
dwellers. What we are now facing is a mass movement of which
both the members and the leaders belong to social classes that are
more humble in origin, far less well educated and with much
stronger roots in the rural sector.

Social mobility has also had an impact on current language and
expressions as well as on the context of popular culture. The
younger generation now use words and expressions that were not in
current use thirty or forty years ago except by the rural population
and lower income urban dwellers, while the President of Egypt
came to be referred to as the 'Rayes', a word previously used
mainly to refer to a craftsman. The long, elaborate and often
sophisticated songs gave way to much shorter songs with lighter
tunes and easier words. In the cinema, television and theatre, the
old plots which long dominated the content of films and plays are
also giving way to new plots where poverty is no longer associated
with honesty and wealth with vice, nor is access to wealth confined
to the very unlikely coincidence of a rich man falling in love with a
poor girl or a poor man suddenly discovering a hidden and
forgotten treasure. The most popular of the new films and plays
now treat the access to wealth as an entirely possible and normal

occurrence but often make fun of the customs, styles of life and manners of expression of the older and declining upper classes.

Side by side with the gradual rise of popular culture there is also an increasing tendency towards the westernisation of social life and daily patterns of living. This process of increasing westernisation is by no means a new phenomenon of social development in Egypt, where it has for at least a century served as a symbol of social advancement. What is new is that westernisation is increasingly becoming a process of 'Americanisation', adopted by the younger generation far more than by their elders, and reflected much more in outward behaviour and external appearances than in ways of thinking and moral values. For borrowing from the 'west' no longer stands for borrowing from 'Europe', and exposure to the west no longer takes place mainly through going to school, or through books, the radio, or the press but rather through the cinema and television or through direct contact with tourists and foreigners abroad.

Conclusion

While there is much to lament in the impact of rapid social mobility on Egypt's economic and social life, it is possible to see some important reasons for optimism with regard to its ultimate impact on the future economic development of Egypt. So many of the psychological ills that have often been the subject of complaints in the past and which seemed to constitute difficult obstacles in the path towards economic development, may very well have been merely the psychological traits of the upper classes which are now in decline. In contrast, the newly rising classes seem to possess exactly the opposite psychological traits which could prove highly valuable for the future economic reconstruction of Egypt. These rising classes seem to possess a degree of vitality, energy and perseverance which the traditionally upper classes seem to have lacked. They are far more ambitious, less sentimental and often ruthless. In spite of their apparently strong adherence to tradition they are really far less fatalistic in outlook and much more confident in what they can achieve through their own efforts. They would spare nothing for the economic advancement of their children while, for the same reason, they may be much more willing to practise birth control than the traditionally poor or the old upper classes. They are much more conscious of the value of time, have more respect for manual labour and much greater admiration for modern technology. Though much of their new wealth and social advancement has been built on breaking the law, their success in maintaining their new social position may depend on greater discipline and stricter observance of rules. While their rapid advance may have been largely due to a period of 'growth without development', they may very well prove to be the builders of a new era of genuine economic progress.

References

Abdel Khalek G. and Tignor R. eds. (1982), *The political Economy of income distribution in Egypt*, Holmes and Meier, N.Y.

Sorokin P (1959), *Social and cultural mobility*, The Free Press of Glencoe, Illinois.

5

DEBT AND EGYPT'S FINANCIAL POLICIES

David Butter

Background to Egypt's indebtedness

Egypt is in the big league of debtor nations. Its total debt is not far short of $500,000 million, almost as big as Argentina's and half the size of that of league leader Brazil. But despite its impressive size, Egypt's external debt does not present such a serious problem to the international financial community as do the Latin American debtors. This is mainly because the bulk of Egypt's debt is official - owed to governments rather than banks. Much of the debt was contracted on concessionary terms, and the process of rescheduling is that much easier when it involves a handful of major industrial nations rather than dozens of international banks.

But while Egypt may be better off than some other debtor nations because of the structure of its debt, it is far worse off in other respects. South Korea is often cited as a prime example of a developing country borrowing heavily to build a sound basis for export-led growth. Whatever reservations one might have about holding up the Korean experience as a model for development, the contrast with Egypt is remarkable. Apart from some notable improvements to the economy's infrastructure, Egypt's massive borrowing has done little to ease the country's dependence on two key exports: oil and labour.

As Egypt's debt has grown inexorably larger, and the burden of servicing the debt more difficult to bear, the government has been obliged to consider radical measures to deal with the problem. This has entailed, first and foremost, dealing with the International Monetary Fund (IMF). In May 1987, Egypt agreed an economic reform package with the IMF, which is providing a SDR 250 million standby credit over 18 months. The IMF deal led to a 10-year rescheduling agreement through the Club of Paris, the informal group of OECD creditor governments. The price of these agreements has been the commitment to an economic reform package, with potentially hazardous political implications. The first issue is nationalism. Egypt was the original Third World debtor, getting into such trouble with its debt in the late 19th century that it had to cede much of its sovereignty to Britain and France. The government is working hard to create the impression that the economic reforms being carried out are not dictated by the IMF, so as to avoid the politically hazardous perception of spendthrift rulers once more pawning Egypt's hard won independence. The second and more immediate issue is the shape the economic reforms will take. They will necessarily entail increases in the cost of living of the poor as efforts are made to increase agricultural productivity and introduce more market mechanisms into the economy. The need to iron out distortions in the state sector of the economy will have to be balanced carefully against the dangers of provoking massive social unrest.

This paper will analyse the structure of Egypt's external debt with relation to the country's main economic indicators; this will be followed by an examination of the options open for dealing with the problems created by the scale of the debt in light of the requirements of the international financial community and the constraints of domestic policy-making.

Egypt: Public Sector Debt 1985-1986

(£E million at official rate of $1 = £E0.70)

	June 1985	June 1986
US	4,555	5,317
W, Europe, Japan and Canada	3,793	6,365
Arab & Islamic countries	2,439	2,503
Comecon Countries and China*	435	665
Australia and other countries	465	599
Arab aid agencies	1,844	1,896
World Bank	859	1,062
IDA	617	671
IMF	241	238
Regional institutions**	284	214
Locally incorporated banks	577	874
Other	788	827
TOTAL	16,898	21,232
Total equivalent in US $	24,125	30,278

Source: Central Bank of Egypt, Cairo

* Debt valued at bilateral accounting rate, which understates the total

** Includes African Development Bank, European Investment Bank and Islamic Development Bank

Egypt: External debt estimates, June 1986

	($ Million)
Public Sector	30,300
-Medium/long term	24,300
-Short term	6,000
Private Sector	2,000
Military Debt	11,000
-US	4,500
-Soviet Union	3,000
-Other Countries	3,500
TOTAL	44,000

Annual debt service (interest and principal): approximately $4,000 million, equivalent to about 40 per cent of current account receipts.

Egypt's external debt has increased dramatically over the past decade. The debt is now estimated at about $40,000 million, excluding loans from the Soviet Union and Eastern Europe. The total figure has risen markedly over the past three years, despite a clampdown on fresh borrowing. The latest increases, however, stem mainly from improved monitoring of the debt and the appreciation of the Japanese yen and the main European currencies against the US dollar. About a quarter of the total debt is made up of military loans, contracted at commercial rates. Half of the military debt is owed to the US, with interest rates fixed at 12-14 per cent, and with severe penalties for payments arrears. Almost one-third of the civilian debt is owed to Western Europe and Japan, mostly in the form of supplier credits and concessionary government loans for projects. Just less than one-fifth of the total civilian debt is owed to Arab and Islamic countries and Arab aid agencies. About $2,000 million is owed to the World Bank and its affiliate, the International Development Agency (IDA). Only about one fifth of the total debt is classified as bilateral or multilateral development aid or military loans.

How did Egypt get itself so heavily into debt? One reason clearly was the shift from the Soviet Union to the US as the main source of military procurement after the October 1973 Arab-Israeli war. Re-equipping the Egyptian armed forces with weapons purchased from the US and Western Europe proved highly expensive. In the late 1970s and early 1980s, Egypt contracted the bulk of its military debt to the US at a time of historically high interest rates. The government chose to finance its purchases of US equipment at fixed rates. The terms, set by the US Treasury, included a four per cent penalty for any arrears and the stipulation that arrears of more than one year should be penalised by a suspension of all aid. Since 1984, the US has been providing military aid of about $1,300 million a year in grant form, but the problem of servicing the existing US military debt has become a heated political issue between Cairo and Washington.

A second reason for Egypt's indebtedness is the substantial investment made in infrastructure projects. President Mubarak and his ministers make repeated reference to the vital projects carried out or underway which required foreign borrowing. The government undoubtedly has a fair point here - few could deny that during the Nasserist era, sectors such as sewerage, telecommunications, irrigation and housing were neglected as Egypt was launched on the road of heavy industry and an ambitious political strategy. Foreign expertise has been essential in carrying out such vast schemes as the Greater Cairo Wastewater Project and the overhaul of the Egyptian telephone system.

Another reason for the debt has been the inability of agricultural production to keep pace with the rise in population. Food output has been growing at about two per cent a year, while the annual rate of population growth is 2.7 per cent. Egypt now runs an agricultural trade deficit of more that $2,000 million a year. The increase in population, combined with the general modernisation of the ecomony, has also entailed a rapid rise in electricity demand, which in turn requires substantial investment in power stations, to be procured from abroad.

Additional factors in the growth in Egypt's external debt are oil wealth and vested interests. Egypt's foreign exchange earnings took off in the mid-1970s with the development of the oil sector and remittances from Egyptian workers in the booming Arab oil - exporting states. Towards the end of the decade, Suez Canal dues and a tourism boom added to the buoyancy of Egypt's foreign exchange earnings. With so much hard currency pouring in, with US aid starting to take on vast proportions and with the Arab states freely disbursing aid, there seemed little reason for concern about Egypt's debt servicing capabilities. And a fast growing economy, with a high propensity to consume, created its own vested interests.

The dramatic fall in oil prices in 1986 concentrated the minds of Egypt's financial policy-makers. In 1985, net oil revenues - exports minus imports - totalled just over $2,600 million. Egypt earns barely half this from its other visible exports. In 1986, net oil revenues fell by 70 per cent to $686 million, a catastrophic loss in earnings caused partly by the authorities' sluggish response to market fluctuations. 1986 also saw a slowdown in tourism - an important source of invisible foreign exchange earnings - because of the February riots in Cairo and Western hysteria about Middle Eastern terrorism. Set against these factors were the vast amounts of foreign exchange being sent back to Egypt in the form of migrant workers' remittances. Official estimates of the total remitted rely on two sources of data: bank transfers and authorised imports carried out with no conversion of currency - such 'own exchange' imports are, of course, financed from the unofficial currency market, fed almost entirely by remittances. The official tally of remittances - which probably understates the total - reached a peak of almost $4,000 million in 1983/84. This fell to about $3,000 million in 1985/86. Of particular concern to the government was that the proportion of bank transfers in total fell in 1986 from about 30 per cent in the early 1980s to barely 10 per cent. But the basic fact is that remittances have resulted in the accumulation of massive private wealth, which surely should play a more significant role in both productive investment and in financing government deficits through such instruments as bond issues. An indicator of the scale of this private wealth is the size of foreign currency bank deposits - more than $8,000 million. In addition, foreign currency deposits in the Islamic investment companies *sharikat tawzif al-amwal* are put at more than $5,000 million.

The government, then, is faced with a crushing external debt servicing burden and vast reservoirs of private wealth, surrounded by the poverty of the mass of Egyptians. The favoured approach to reconciling these problems has been to try to elaborate a strategy of structural reforms to promote the move to what has been termed a 'managed market economy'. But first, the government has been obliged to seek practical relief from its debt servicing burden.

Friends in need

President Mubarak, it must be said, has not fired the imagination of the Egyptian people with his drab message of hard work at home and balance in international relations. But while he has failed to emulate the glory of Nasser and Sadat, he has managed to avoid their disasters. In the field of foreign policy he has scored some quiet but significant achievements, in particular in securing foreign debt relief. The trick has been to emphasise the importance of Egypt remaining politically stable for the interest of a wide range of creditors - the US, West European states, the Soviet Union and the Arab Gulf states.

The pay-off has been an IMF agreement and Paris Club rescheduling with relatively mild terms attached. About $7,500 million in arrears and payments to OECD states has been rescheduled at the Paris Club, together with about $4,500 million in debt payments to Gulf states.

In the bilateral negotiations about external debts, the main issue tended to be military loans. As noted above, military debt accounts for about 25 per cent of Egypt's total borrowing, and a substantially higher proportion of total debt servicing. Servicing the military debt to the US takes up a staggering 30 per cent of total interest payments - some $650 million a year out of an annual total of about $2,200 million. The US military debt is of vital importance, but it is, unfortunately, one area where Mubarak's assiduous efforts have so far failed to yield tangible results. Egypt has pressed the US to reduce the interest rates on the military loans either to a reasonable fixed level - of, say, seven per cent - or to current floating rates from the high fixed rates of 12-14 per cent at which the loans were contracted in 1979-84. Washington has refused to do this because of the danger perceived in setting a precedent. Egypt is one of the largest debtors suffering from the burden of high fixed rates on US treasury loans, but it is by no means the only one. There are about 38 countries around the world with similar problems; there are also US farmers, with an aggregate debt of more than $100,000 million contracted at the high interest rates prevailing in the late 1970s and early 1980s. If Egypt received preferential treatment, there would be pressure for concessions to be made to the other debtors, a prospect unwelcome to the US treasury department - with its own vast fiscal deficit to deal with. Another option is private sector refinancing of the US military debt. Two major US banks - one specialising in debt swap from fixed to floating interest rates, the other with expertise in refinancing debts through bond issues - have carefully studied the question, and are keen to take on the Egyptian military debt to the US. But the private sector solution is impractical without US government guarantees. These have not been forthcoming.

In late 1986, the US proposed two options available to countries facing difficulty in servicing their US military debts. One option was cash prepayment. This was attractive to relatively wealthy countries, such as Spain, but not feasible for Egypt. To prepay the $4,550 million debt, Egypt would have had to borrow the amount. The only body suitable to guarantee such a loan is the US government: the prepayment option specifically excluded the possibility of US guarantees being provided for fresh borrowing.

The other option entailed interest rates being cut to about seven and a half per cent for a four-year period. But the difference between the reduced rate and the original rate would be refinanced. None of the original interest charges would be forgiven, and in addition, the borrower would have to pay the extra charges for the refinancing on the loans' maturity in 2009-2014. The government has calculated that this option would add around $5,000 million to the aggregate interest of just below $10,000 million on the whole US military debt. In the event, the US military debt is being dealt with in the Paris Club deal. But this will still entail substantial extra servicing costs for Egypt in the future.

In the absence of a long term solution to the problem, the two sides have had to resort to short term remedies. This entails the somewhat absurd process of a cheque for a few hundred million dollars being drafted by the US treasury department as an instalment on the US military debt. US non-military aid totals about $815 million. It was intended that these funds be disbursed by the US Agency for International Development (USAID) as grants for projects - such as the Cairo, Alexandria and Canal cities wastewater schemes and the rehabilitation of the Aswan High Dam - or for financing imports from the US of commodities such as railway locomotives. In 1985, US congress authorised a $500 million cash supplement to the aid budget, so that the transfers needed for the military debt could be met without affecting the normal aid activities. However, US budget constraints in 1986 meant that such supplements would not be repeated. The only recourse has been to turn the bulk of the capital aid budget into cash transfers. This is not too drastic in the short term because of delays in disbursing aid funds - there are sufficient funds already in the pipeline to keep USAID projects going for some years to come. Since 1984, the US has also been providing about $1,300 million a year in grants for military purchases. Egypt has to set its frustration with Washington's inflexibility on existing military debts against the fact that in 1987, for example, Cairo was able to place an order for forty advanced F-16 fighter aircraft valued at $1,300 million in total, all of which will be covered by a grant.

An additional problem with US military debt is that it is not liable to what might be termed 'unilateral rescheduling' - or simply building up arrears. As noted above, there is a penalty of four per cent for any payments delays on the US military debt; arrears of more than twelve months are penalised by the suspension of all aid. For the foreseeable future, there seems little prospect of any comprehensive solution to the military debt issue; in the meantime, the US treasury will continue to have to meet the bulk of the Egyptian interest payments.

West European military debt also poses problems for Egypt, but of more manageable proportions. The main problem countries are France and Spain, owed about $2,000 million and $850 million respectively for military orders. Serious payments problems began to surface in 1985. Measures were taken by both France and Spain to ease the payments schedule. France agreed to spread out delivery of twenty Mirage 2000 fighter aircraft; Spain agreed to a one-year moratorium on some payments, subject to suitable downpayments being made. Spain had already reacted to the arrears by scaling down the size of the original orders. Military trucks destined for Egypt were simply reallocated to the Spanish army. By mid-1986, France and Spain had decided that the only way to deal with the arrears on their military debt was to refer it to the Paris Club along with the rest of Egypt's external debt. In early 1987, France effectively cancelled export credit cover for Egypt and suspended delivery of the final batch of six Mirages. This was a clear signal that there was no longer any scope for bilateral rescheduling.

By contrast, early 1987 saw the completion of a bilateral agreement between Egypt and the Soviet Union about military debts estimated to total about $3,000 million. While a significant pointer towards a warming in Soviet-Egyptian relations after the ructions of the Sadat era, the debt rescheduling was not quite the coup that it might seem at first sight. It merely formalised the situation whereby Egypt had simply not been paying the two per cent interest on the debt. The agreement entailed cancelling the interest charge, and rescheduling payments over 25 years, including six years' grace. The Soviet side agreed to the rescheduling on condition that a solution is found to the bilateral trade problem, in particular the grossly overvalued exchange rate used. The rate was £1 sterling = £E 0.70. This values the Egyptian pound at treble the official commercial bank rate, and more than four times the free market rate. The rate effectively meant that Soviet importers had to pay grossly inflated prices, while the Egyptian farmer or public sector industry received a pittance for goods purchased by state agencies for exports to the Soviet Union. The rate has since been revalued to £1 sterling = £E 2.00, but this is still well below the market rate.

The other area where there is still scope for bilateral rescheduling is with regard to Arab loans. Egypt owes more than $5,000 million to Arab and Islamic countries and Arab aid agencies. Like the Soviet debt, little of this debt has been serviced for some years. This is mainly because of the breach in diplomatic relations with Arab countries after Egypt signed its peace treaty with Israel in 1979. However, one of the pay-offs of the steady rapprochement with Arab countries during Mubarak's rule is that a substantial portion of the Arab debt is effectively being written off according to the Paris Club deal.

The Arab factor is also of relevance in considering one of the most glaring questions with regard to Egypt's external debt: why is such a large part of the debt made up of military loans? The answer to this question was suggested, in part, above when reference was made to the shift of Egypt's military procurement from East to West. But an equally important factor is the large measure of autonomy enjoyed by the military in Egypt. The armed forces run a wide range of industries, mostly geared to military production. Exports of military material, in particular to Iraq, have generated large foreign currency earnings for the armed forces. These earnings have enabled the military to finance much of its weapons purchases. The precise relationship between the military and the strictly civilian part of the government is complex, and it is beyond the scope of this chapter to unravel it. Even in the specific field of external debt it is difficult to say conclusively how much of the military loan repayments have been made by the military. By the same token, there are no figures available for the size of the military's foreign currency earnings, and through what institutions those earnings are channelled. Even the size of the defence budget is a matter for conjecture rather than public record. Any observations in this regard are therefore, of necessity, tentative and based on various unverifiable sources of inside information.

What can be said with a fair degree of confidence is that the Gulf war has created a lucrative market for Egyptian military materials. In the first instance, Egypt sold to Iraq large quantities of stockpiled spare parts and equipment dating from the time when Egypt's army was Soviet-equipped - the Soviet Union is also the largest weapons supplier to Iraq. Subsequently, Egypt's military industries supplied Iraq with a range of items, from Tucano training aircraft produced from Brazilian kits, to the Fahd and Walid armoured vehicles adapted from Soviet originals. Iraq was also sold vast quantities of Egyptian-made ammunition. Revenues from these sales have been anything from $500 million to $1,000 million a year. It became apparent in 1985 that the military ran into difficulty with its debt servicing payments - perhaps because of Iraqi payments delays, perhaps because of the increase in Egypt's military debt servicing burden. Reports at this time suggested that the central bank was asked to meet military debt obligations of which it was previously ignorant. By 1987, when an Iraqi military collapse began to seem a distinct possibility, reports surfaced about Saudi and Kuwaiti involvement in paying Egypt for its military supplies to Iraq. According to some bankers, this Saudi and Kuwaiti involvement also included a form of subsidy to Egypt, as the prices paid for the supplies to Iraq were said to be double or treble the real value of the equipment. While it must be emphasised that hard facts about such transactions are difficult to come by, it is evident that the Arab Gulf states see Egypt as a potential counterweight to Iranian the event of Tehran scoring an outright or relative victory in the Gulf war. It is, therefore, worth investing in Egypt's stability. Despite the scope for bilateral solutions to the debt problem, Egypt has finally been obliged to deal with a large portion of its debt through the relevant international institutions, first and foremost the IMF. Negotiations with the IMF began in earnest in mid-1986, when the government finally accepted that, with the collapse in oil revenues, multilateral rescheduling was inescapable.

The government succeeded in getting the IMF to approve a relatively modest economic reform programme. The key element was the exchange rate. In an uncharacteristically smooth operation, on 10 May a new free market exchange rate - competitive with the previously dominant black market rate was unveiled. Black market dealers were arrested, and steps were taken to dampen demand for foreign currency through issuing credit ceilings for banks and tightening up the rules for issuing letters of credit. The government endeavoured to protect consumers from the effect of what amounted to an almost 40 per cent devaluation by decreeing that imports of basic goods - about 60 per cent of total imports - should be calculated at stronger rates for the Egyptian pound. The new system worked reasonably well in its first months of operation, partly because a surge in tourism boosted the supply of foreign exchange coming into the country. But doubts have persisted about how transition to a private sector dominated by the official bank economy can be achieved while the parallel economy remains so powerful. The main locus of power of the parallel sector is the Islamic investment companies, which have provided attractive returns to depositors because the official deposit rate has kept lower than inflation.

The government also agreed to follow IMF advice on lifting energy subsidies and removing distortions in the pricing of agricultural produce, but it baulked at following IMF recommendations to free interest rates.

The IMF deal encouraged the Paris Club, where the group of 18 creditor governments agreed to reschedule arrears outstanding as of December 1986 and interest and principal payments due on government and government-guaranteed loans falling due between January 1987 and June 1988. The total package - which covered civilian and military debts - came to about $12,000 million, including roughly $4,500 million owed to Arab Gulf states. The details of the rescheduling were hammered out between Egypt and the individual creditors. Cairo will have eventually to meet the cost of fresh borrowing by the creditor governments to compensate for the deferral of Egypt's debt servicing payments. Egypt has been obliged to accept that these refinancing costs are to be at market rather than concessional rates.

The IMF/Paris Club arrangements have been something of a triumph for Egypt in that the government has secured reasonably soft terms for coping with the debt problem. However, it is a temporary solution, and Cairo is now locked in to what promises to be an interminable process of draining negotiations about payment deferments for debts already rescheduled. There is also likely to come a point at which Egypt and the IMF have serious disagreements about policy implementation. Cairo will be faced with the choice of submitting to more stringent IMF measures, with the ever present risk of sparking popular unrest, or of being ostracised by the international financial community on which it is growing increasingly dependent.

6

EGYPT: SOME ISSUES IN AGRICULTURAL SECTOR POLICY

Simon Commander

Introduction

The primary constraint on raising agricultural production in Egypt remains land. Barely three per cent of the total land area is available for production. Efforts to achieve extensive growth have, over the last three decades, centred on land reclamation. Between 1965-1980 as much as 63 per cent of the agricultural investment budget was allocated to reclamation. By the early 1980s this share had fallen to around 25 per cent, reflecting, in part, the shift of emphasis towards greater intensification of production.

This shift in priorities can, in part, be attributed to the relatively poor results from land reclamation efforts. Since the early 1960s around 1.1 million acres have been brought into production but only a third of this area has managed to cover variable production costs.[1] With urban and other encroachment possibly accounting for an annual loss of 0.45 per cent of the cultivated area, there may now be a net annual loss in the area available for agricultural production.

The factors explaining the poor performance of reclamation projects are various. They include high initial reclamation costs, low productivity of reclaimed land, an absence of complementary infrastructural investment, lack of agronomic experimentation on desert soils, as well as factors concerned with ownership and

137

organisation. However, even when relatively small-scale, private reclamation efforts have occurred, as in the Northern Lakes, financial and economic feasibility tests yield ambiguous results for the available technologies.[2] Moreover, although such initiatives depend strongly on parallel, infrastructural public investment, their feasibility remains more robust than that of the larger state reclamation projects. The latter's relatively poor record has been further compromised by strong labour constraints, the result of the rising wage trend of the most recent period.

Given these factors, the paper starts from the assumption that the net, marginal impact of new land reclamation on agricultural output will remain limited at least over the short and medium term. Emphasis is placed on the use of extant factors of production, where factor substitutions, as policy and reality, are concentrated on capital and labour. In particular, the paper is concerned with the relative price structure facing agricultural producers and the effect of government price interventions on resource allocation and, specifically, the technical mix in agricultural production.

Constraints on agricultural production

The overall performance of the agricultural sector in the recent period has been weak. Sectoral growth rates averaged around 3.5 per cent through the 1970s, falling to below 2.5 per cent between 1980-1983/84. In the same period the economy as a whole grew by around eight per cent per annum. The relatively poor record of agriculture can be attributed not only to the land constraint but also the failure to raise productivity levels. While inadequate attention to drainage and salinity problems, as well as institutional weaknesses in the delivery of services to agriculturalists, are commonly cited factors behind these trends, the Government has also chosen to emphasise the emergence of a strong labour constraint, an apparent symptom of which has been the strong rise in agricultural wages since 1973/74. Interpreted as a scarcity of labour, particularly at peak seasons, this has been associated with an explicit policy stance favouring the substitution of capital for labour.[3] In a Hicksian framework, such a conjucture would induce entrepreneurs and producers to seek out labour-saving innovations. In the Egyptian context, technology innovation has not been the issue. The technology frontier has been given exogenously. The policy stance of the Government has thus involved certain decisions regarding the importation or local production of extant technology. In addition, the price of capital, let alone goods and inputs, has been regulated by the Government so as to shift relative prices to favour the adoption of mechanical technology by farmers. Such policies have been formulated with the explicit aim of substituting capital for labour in production, and have attracted considerable external donor financing.

Real wages in agriculture

The apparent shift from a condition of chronic labour abundance to one of shortage may appear surprising given widely held assumptions about the Egyptian labour market. The most accessible indicator of this transformation has been the wage rate in agriculture.

Table 1 presents nominal and real wage rate trends for adult males and child labour in agriculture over the period of 1973-1986. Between 1973 and 1985 real wages rose by over three and a third times. Note, however, that this official time-series suggests a decline in the real wage in 1986.

Table 1: **Agricultural Wage Trends, Egypt 1973 - 1986: Official Ministry of Agriculture Data**

Year	Money Wage	Money Wage Index (1973=100)	Consumer Price Index-Rural	Real Wage Index (1973 = 100)
Adult Males				
1973	28.5	100	100	100
1974	35.1	123	114	108
1975	46.5	163	128	127
1976	61.6	216	143	151
1977	76.0	267	157	170
1978	90.0	316	181	174
1979	107.0	375	192	195
1980	137.0	481	240	200
1981	181.0	635	273	233
1982	235.0	825	311	265
1983	309.0	1084	386	281
1984	383.0	1344	421	319
1985	443.0	1554	470	331
1986*	477.0	1674	539	311
Boys				
1973	13.5	100	100	100
1974	16.7	124	114	109
1975	21.0	156	128	122
1976	28.2	209	143	146
1977	36.3	269	157	171
1978	42.6	316	181	175
1979	47.7	353	192	184
1980	60.6	449	240	187
1981	82.1	608	273	223
1982	107.0	793	311	255
1983	147.0	1088	386	282
1984	192.0	1422	421	338
1985	207.0	1533	470	326
1986*	241.0	1785	539	331

*January-July, 1986

Source: Ministry of Agriculture, A.R.E.

The real wage trend presented in Table 1 suffers from a number of problems. Firstly, the data are highly aggregative, both by region and task, secondly, they do not include wage rates for female labour and, lastly, the consumer price deflator is a conservative estimate of inflation in rural areas. Other survey-generated information suggests that there is in fact a wide spread of labour prices with strong variations in the wage level by region and even village.[4] In other words, there is no one converging price for labour. Nevertheless, these data do confirm the fact of a general real wage increase for adult male labour from the mid-1970s onwards. This real wage increase has, moreover, been substantial, though rather below the rate of increase shown by the official series. The trend for adult female labour and child labour has been less clear and in some areas it appears that real wages for adult women may have remained broadly constant over the same period.

Evidence on the evolution of relative wages by sector is less easy to compile. Between 1974 and 1980/81, the real wage, measured in terms of consumer goods per person employed, increased in agriculture at a rate superior to all other sectors of the economy, bar petroleum.[5] However, the wage differential still remained strong so that in the early 1980s, construction labour, for example, still commanded an average real income between three and five times that for agricultural labour. This indicates that the wage trend in agriculture was not simply determined, as is often argued, by labour supply constraints within the sector, but should be seen as part of a more general wage-push effect in the economy.

Developments within the agricultural sector since the mid-1970s suggest that the strong upward trend in real wages can be explained more by supply-side factors than by shifts in labour demand. Indeed, the latter appears to have remained broadly constant, possibly declining somewhat with the general shift towards fodder crops. Emigration to other Arab states, continuing out-migration to Cairo and other cities, as well as the growth of non-farm employment opportunities in rural areas, are among the major factors cited in explaining the contraction in the supply of labour to agriculture. It should be noted that this contraction almost uniquely applies to adult male labour.

While out-migration, domestic and external, has been a major factor, its importance may, in fact, be greater in relation to, first, employment expectations and, secondly, with regard to the availability of investible resources. This latter factor is of importance in explaining the more rapid diffusion of mechanical technology in the recent period. Of greater significance for the availability of labour for agriculture has been the provision of education and the growth of government and public sector employment. In a labour market survey carried out in three Delta villages in 1984, it was found that, when excluding students, of the effective primary male labour force, slightly under 40 per cent of the sample were farmers, a further 15 per cent were agricultural labourers, under 10 per cent were employed in the non-agricultural private sector and nearly a third of the sample was employed in one way or another by the state.[6] Consequently, for a major share of the male labour force, on-farm work had emerged as a secondary occupation, a feasible strategy given the small average size of Egyptian farms and the growing substitution of female and child labour for male labour.

Table 2: **Production Costs Disaggregated: Major Field Crops 1972-1983: All Egypt**

CROP	72/3	73/4	74/5	80/1	81/2	82/3	83/4	84/85
Cotton								
Rent	33.0	30.0	25.2	20.2	17.2	14.8	10.7	9.9
Wages	31.9	35.6	39.3	50.8	54.4	56.0	59.3	60.0
Draught Power	3.5	3.9	3.2	2.5	2.2	2.4	1.5	1.3
Machinery	6.5	6.4	6.3	6.1	8.0	7.2	8.7	8.3
Material Inputs	23.6	22.7	24.0	17.9	15.4	16.6	15.5	15.5
Other Costs	1.5	1.4	2.0	2.5	2.8	3.0	4.3	5.0
Wheat								
Rent	36.8	35.9	28.8	34.3	29.9	25.9	19.9	14.9
Wages	17.2	17.0	22.3	26.7	27.5	29.1	38.1	41.1
Draught Power	8.7	8.5	5.9	6.8	6.8	5.3	5.0	5.2
Machinery	10.6	10.8	16.2	13.0	14.4	16.3	15.6	17.7
Material Inputs	25.1	25.6	24.2	16.5	18.4	19.0	15.8	16.3
Other Costs	1.6	2.2	2.6	2.7	3.0	4.4	5.9	4.8
Rice								
Rent	23.4	23.0	21.1	16.9	14.0	12.6	11.6	10.0
Wages	26.2	27.9	31.3	34.8	40.0	46.0	45.5	48.6
Draught Power	8.3	7.0	7.3	10.1	8.5	5.7	3.6	5.6
Machinery	14.5	15.0	14.8	14.0	12.8	13.6	19.0	14.6
Material Inputs	26.9	25.6	22.6	20.5	20.3	17.6	15.1	13.4
Other Costs	0.7	1.5	2.9	3.7	4.4	4.5	5.2	7.8
Maize								
Rent	27.9	26.0	25.2	19.9	17.3	17.1	12.8	11.8
Wages	25.2	27.7	30.6	37.5	40.8	41.8	45.1	47.9
Draught Power	8.5	8.5	7.5	6.4	5.5	4.9	3.3	0.9
Machinery	5.8	6.9	6.7	8.5	9.0	10.4	14.3	15.2
Material Inputs	31.4	30.1	28.0	22.3	22.4	21.0	20.4	20.1
Other Costs	1.2	1.8	2.0	5.4	5.0	4.8	4.1	4.1

Material Inputs = seeds, organic/chemical fertilizer and pesticides

Source: Ministry of Agriculture, A.R.E.

Sharp increases in real wages for adult male labour have driven up the labour factor share in aggregate production costs. Table 2, using official data, confirms this point. The table also suggests that machine costs have risen at the expense of draught power. However, it should be noted that these calculations have been made imputing shadow wages to family labour. Survey generated production cost data point to rather lower labour shares, both using nominal and shadow costing. However, on average, for a standard two-season rotation, labour costs varied between 45-60 per cent of total costs. This represents an increased share when compared with the pre-1970 situation. One result has been that aggregate production costs have increased for most of the major field crops at a higher rate than inflation and producer prices. Consequently, there has been a profit squeeze. The response of the Government, strongly supported by the larger farmers, has been to accelerate the adoption of machinery.

Recent Mechanisation   Policy

The case for capital substitution rests on a number of strong assumptions and, in part, on some debatable propositions regarding recent developments in the sector. First, it is assumed that there is a physical shortage of labour that leads to direct productivity losses through non-timely planting and other tasks, as well as stimulating non-optimal crop mixes. Secondly, it is assumed that such labour shortages are now structural, general and non-reversible. Thirdly, it is argued that machine introduction has two major benefits. In the first place, mechanical energy supplants draught power, hence lowering the level of animal stocks and weakening the fodder constraint on Egyptian farms. In the second place, machine use supplants human labour, thereby reducing production costs. It is also commonly argued that machine use has a direct productivity effect. Lower cost, increased output would then have positive implications for both the balance of payments, given Egypt's current requirement to import food, and, at the same time, would drive down the price of wage goods for urban consumers, with a corresponding impact on the underlying price level and trend.

These arguments are problematic. Take the proposition regarding productivity and crop mix. It is true that most Egyptian farmers dispense with a second picking of the cotton crop and possibly practice a poorer quality husbandry with regard to this crop. Furthermore, an increasing number of farmers are prepared to defy area controls and plant crops other than cotton, even if this involves paying a fine. Such decisions are in part motivated by labour market conditions. Labour factor shares for cotton are significantly higher than for other crops. However, this is a question as much related to the tax structure - and hence farmgate prices - for particular crops as it is to labour charges.

Historically, Egyptian farmers have been relatively steeply taxed through both a land tax and implicit taxation through administered prices.[7] In the latter regard, such implicit taxation has concentrated particularly on the major tradable, cotton . By the mid-1970s such taxation resulted in reductions in agricultural producer incomes of around LE 1.2 billion; 85 per cent of this transfer being towards consumers, the remainder being a direct transfer to the Exchequer.[8] Since then, the taxation rate has declined. By 1980 the total burden on agriculture was less than 20 per cent of the peak level of 1974, when measured in constant 1975 prices. This yielded an indirect tax of around 17 per cent.[9] Other computations place the figure at a slightly lower level - 14 per cent in 1981.[10]

For cotton, one simple measure of the implicit taxation is the discrepancy between procurement and border prices calculated with a weighted average exchange rate. Between 1970-1984 producers received on average a little over half the border price for their output. One result was that controlled domestic crop prices (i.e. for cotton, rice, beans and, at times, wheat) rose over this period at a rate consistently inferior to that of the non-regulated crops and fodder crops, in particular. With effective protection given to meat production, there was thus a strong shift in relative profitability in favour of livestock products, a further stimulant to the cultivation of fodder and, most particularly, birseem. Thus, from a level of around nineteen per cent of the cropped area in the early 1950s, cotton accounted for around ten per cent by the early 1980s.

In other words, forced deliveries and administered prices have not only blocked a move towards greater regional specialisation and generated suboptimal land allocations, but have also failed to achieve the major goals of such interventions. Farm households have moved into the production of non-controlled crops where private returns have been higher. The lower labour input requirements characteristic of the major fodder crops, birseem, may have assisted this process, at least since the mid-1970s. However, it needs to be noted that vegetable and fruit production, other areas where increases have been pronounced, have relatively higher labour requirements. As regards productivity, it can also be noted that cotton productivity has risen more sharply than for other crops, again rather undermining the view that labour shortages have had a detrimental productivity effect. In short, shifts in the crop mix away from traditional tradables such as cotton, towards home goods, reflects not only the buoyancy of domestic demand, given income and population effects, but also the price signals operating in the economy. Partial price and output interventions by the State are far more significant in explaining the output structure than the trend in the real agricultural wage rate. The wedge between economic and private returns that characterises the present crop mix could be better adjusted through producer price increments than through shifts in the technical framework of production, especially where such shifts are generally unlikely to be crop-specific.

There is a further strand in the argument for capital substitution in agriculture that is of dubious merit. This relates to the critical supposition that there is a labour shortage. Four points can be made in this context. In the first instance, labour scarcity has to be discussed in terms of the shift in relative factor prices. Secondly, seasonal tightening of the labour market is not a novel feature in Egyptian agriculture. Thirdly, tightening in the labour market has been largely for adult male labour and has been met with a widespread substitution of female and child labour for adult males. In crop production, total female and child labour, both hired and household, now accounts for between 28-33 per cent of total labour time. Moreover, as non-farm employment opportunities for males have grown and livestock work has engaged a growing share of on-farm female household labour-time, Egyptian farmers have increasingly hired in labour for crop work. For the major tasks that pose supply bottlenecks - for example, rice transplanting and cotton picking - such hired labour has mainly been female or child. In other words, there is a strong labour market in rural areas to which the majority of small farm households have recourse, both as hirers and sellers. Fourthly, despite greater year-round tightness in the supply of male labour, the market for such agricultural labour is not a clearing market. Official statistics estimate very low unemployment rates (3.2 per cent in 1981) in rural areas.[11] As before, the real issue is under-employment.[12] Available evidence suggests that there is continuing seasonal under-employment for male labour in rural areas and this is likely to be more pronounced in areas furthest away from towns and communications. So if the labour market cannot clear, except at peak periods, with high government labour demand and emigration, this again casts doubt on strategies designed to lower the demand for labour in agriculture.

A further point needs to be made with regard to the issue of labour scarcity. Reductions in the supply of male labour to agriculture have come about not only as a function of education, but also on account of emigration and, most particularly, the growth in government and public sector employment. In the latter regard, the last national labour force sample survey (1981) estimated that nearly thirty per cent of the male labour force was employed by the state. Moreover, nearly a third of such jobs were in rural areas. Consequent upon this precocious growth in government employment have been problems of overstaffing, low pay and poor morale. In addition, this has placed growing pressure on the government budget. Between 1979 and 1984 wages as a share of current government expenditure rose from 23 per cent to 27 per cent, further fuelling the size of the budget deficit.[13]

Yet, employment opportunities outside of Egypt are declining and are likely to continue to decline. With a labour force growing at over two and a half per cent per annum, enhanced substitution of capital for labour in a sector which accounts for nearly two-fifths of the total labour force, would have major, longer term implications. In other words, if past practice were to be replicated this would mean either a continuing growth in government employment - itself an undesirable aim - or else a very sharp increase in the labour absorbing capacity of the private manufacturing and services sectors. Given current relative prices and the investment framework (including Law 43) a shift to more labour intensive production in the industrial sector cannot be assumed. Reducing agriculture's ability to act as a labour reservoir consequently assumes a set of parallel responses in other sectors that are either undesirable or unfeasible.

With regard to other parallel arguments for accelerating the adoption of mechanical technology, similar doubts can be raised. Clearly, the adoption of labour saving technologies will be largely a rising function of the wage rate. Most available evidence from a range of country studies suggests that productivity effects, through increased yields, will be rarely associated with mechanisation per se but would be contingent on the further adoption of new technical packages, such as improved seeds. Thus, the main mechanism promoting mechanisation would be through the reduction of unit costs. In addition, other more subjective factors, like reduction in drudgery, could play a partial role in determining technology choice.

In Egypt, the cost reduction argument works relatively well in explaining the rapid diffusion of tractors and threshers over the past fifteen years. At the same time, the opportunity cost of draught animal use has been an important factor. With protection for domestic meat production, output has increased by around 20 per cent between 1974/75 and 1983/84. At the same time, stocks of cattle and buffaloes have risen. Substitution of mechanical for animal energy in production has enabled a release of livestock holdings to meat and dairy production. This has raised the demand for fodder and hence reduced the supply of tradables, let alone food crops. As regards labour substitution, extensive mechanisation of land preparation, irrigation and threshing has undoubtedly reduced the demand for male labour in particular. Yet, the truly labour intensive tasks - weeding and harvesting - have as yet been little mechanised. The key aim of government policy has been to remedy this situation.

The Economics of Mechanisation

The path to a full mechanisation of Egyptian agriculture has remained problematic. First, technological solutions have, in certain key cases, been evasive. Adequate mechanical picking technology for Egyptian long and extra-long staple cotton has not been developed. For rice, small Japanese combines have been introduced for both transplanting and harvesting, but these have posed adaptive problems and have not been accompanied by a suitable, wider technical package.

The labour substituting properties of such technology illustrate, however, the longer run employment implications of such a shift in production technique. For both transplanting and harvesting of rice, machine use would require a complementary labour input of between 7-16 per cent of that for manual technology. Introduction of mower-binders for wheat or birseem would likewise reduce labour demand by around 75-80 per cent. The substitution effect would be highly significant.[14]

To estimate the likely costs and benefits of such machine introduction requires considering not only the opportunity cost of released labour but also the direct foreign exchange and other indirect costs associated with the diffusion of machinery. In other words, much will depend on the relationship between the shadow cost of foreign exchange, the domestic opportunity cost of labour, the direct incremental output effect associated with the capital/labour substitution and the impact on production unit costs. Let us deal with each in turn.

Valuation of foreign exchange has been made complex by the adherence to a set of exchange pools. Nevertheless, it seems that between 1979 and mid-1986 the Egyptian pound appreciated by over 50 per cent.[15] One consequence has been to stimulate public sector imports. Concessional lending by major donors, as well as outright grants, has also accelerated the mechanisation programme. In addition, domestic subsidisation of both capital and energy has further skewed the price regimes under which technology choices have in theory been made. Consequently, if foreign exchange, capital and energy were priced at economic rates, the incentive to adoption would fall dramatically. Using 1984 prices, when domestic energy costs were roughly twelve per cent of international levels, tractor operating costs alone showed an upward divergence of between 217-287 per cent over financial operating costs. This level of effective subsidy has been complemented not only by the impact of exchange rate appreciation on the import delivery cost but also by the consistent subsidisation of capital by the State.

Between 1976 and 1986 the interest rate has been significantly negative in real terms when using the central bank discount rate. Since 1983/84 this has remained constant at 13 per cent. Interest rates for machinery purchase have been even lower in nominal terms at 7 per cent. In other words, in most years the interest rate for machine purchase has been negative by around 9-12 per cent, at a conservative estimate.

One implication of the existence of such heavy subsidies is that agricultural projects with a major machinery component have only yielded an acceptable internal rate of return under exceedingly optimistic incremental output scenarios. Consider the case of the World Bank's Second Agricultural Development Project which was approved by the Board in 1985 but which has not, as yet, been drawn on by the Egyptian Government. The project's total cost would (at 1985 prices) amount to US$359 million, of which the foreign exchange cost - largely covered by IBRD - would comprise US$179 million. Apart from importation of a range of agricultural machinery, including tractors, levellers, binders, combines and so on, the project would aim to establish machinery repair and service facilities, mechanisation centres for demonstration and testing of new machines as well as improvements to extension and credit services to farmers. The project coverage would extend to seven

Delta governorates with a final coverage of around 650,000 farmers. Farm machinery costs comprised over 60 per cent of foreign exchange costs and 40 per cent of total base costs for the project.[16]

Justification for this and other mechanisation projects has ultimately been made on two counts. First, through cost reduction on account of labour substitution. Secondly, through direct yield effects through improved practices. In general, the latter effect has assumed complementary development of agronomic packages, although in some cases yield effects have been attributed (erroneously, for the most part) directly to machine adoption. In the case of the Second Agricultural Development project the critical variable determining project viability would be the higher level of cropping intensification that would, in theory, be associated with machine adoption. The project document cites an intensity shift from 1.9 to 1.95, a direct function of labour saving. At the same time, average yields were estimated to rise by between 20-40 per cent for the major crops. In addition, it was assumed that adult farm labour shortages were a growing phenomenon.

Apart from the optimistic assumptions regarding output, it can be argued that recent mechanisation projects have ignored a number of salient facts. In the first place, further mechanisation of agriculture involves displacing largely female and child labour.

It can be argued that the opportunity cost may not be that high, unless strong assumptions are made regarding, first, the value of education and, secondly, the dynamic, economy-wide effects on the demand for children at household level.[17] Furthermore, there has been the assumption that adult male wage rates were a true reflection of the trend in *all* wage rates within the sector. Moreover, it has been assumed that the rate of increment between 1973/74 and 1985 would be sustained. Yet, already by 1986 real wage rates for adult males had fallen. The foreign exchange cost of such projects has tended to be underestimated and a realistic set of economic prices for capital and energy have, in some instances, not been applied. The upward adjustment in domestic energy prices of between 60-80 per cent in May 1987 and the devaluation of the pound will radically change the cost structure under which the choice of technology must be made. This will clearly reduce the attraction of substituting capital for labour.

A final point needs to be made regarding the current policy of the Government with regard to mechanisation. This concerns the institutional component. A number of detailed studies have demonstrated that, for the most part, it has been the private sector that has provided tractors, threshers, irrigation pumps and transporters to farmers.[18] In general, few farmers have purchased such equipment, relying instead on a fluent custom-hire market. This has been stimulated not only by subsidised capital and running costs but also by the multi-purpose capacity of the major machine type, the tractor. There is evidence that return migrants have invested in such machine acquisition, given the likely level of returns from the custom-hire market. As more owners have entered this market the hire price has declined in real terms, by about 10 per cent between 1977 and 1984 in parts of the Delta. Yet, despite this, the State has entered the custom-hire market through the establishment of Agricultural Mechanisation Centres run by the Ministry of Agriculture. These institutions have been largely funded directly by the State with some external donor assistance for initial stocking of machinery. For the most part, such machines have comprised tractors, ploughs and a variety of rice combines. Hiring-out of machinery has been conducted at financial rates roughly half current market rates for machine hire from the private sector. This has been done on the assumption that such rates are too high but the level of machine stocks for such Centres suggest that their ability to influence the market price would be very limited. In addition, these centres have been set up with the aim of demonstrating new technologies and accelerating their adoption. While this might be desirable if it could be established that there was indeed a strong, economic case for further mechanisation, it raises the question as to why the public sector needs to be involved, especially given the high overhead costs associated with the initiative. Previous experience with cooperative (gamiya) ownership of tractors and other implements has been a poor one and there are few reasons for supposing that this will not be repeated with the present Mechanisation Centres.

Conclusion: Some Policy Options

In the recent past Egyptian agriculture has been marked both by a relatively low rate of growth and by a range of problems relating to the impact of particular price interventions. Tradables production has suffered not only through the trade and exchange regime but also on account of domestic pricing policy. Producers have shifted into fodder crops, specifically birseem and maize. Even wheat has been largely cultivated for its straw. Apart from reducing aggregate cotton output and hence potential foreign exchange revenues for the government, a further consequence has been the declining share of domestic food consumption that has been satisfied by local production. This has been a function not only of the current structure of returns to particular crops but also has been a consequence of the growth in consumption levels that has accompanied a relatively high overall growth rate since the mid-1970s. In addition, the extensive food subsidy systems have had a major impact on effective demand for food items. By and large, the subsidy system appears not to have been financed through low producer prices. However, that system has required far higher levels of food imports. By 1981/82 food imports exceeded by some five times the sum of export revenues from cotton and other agricultural exports. Between 1978 and 1983 wheat alone comprised around 6.5 per cent of the total cost of commodity imports. Thus, increased food imports, in part financed by concessional means and by co-opted revenues, have been contemporaneous with a fall in export earnings from agricultural trade.[19]

To address these issues will clearly require a range of policies, including a macro-economic framework more suitable to sustaining growth in tradables production. At the same time, it is evident that budgetary constraints will necessarily impose limitations on public expenditure commitments in agriculture. Precisely because public investment in the sector has tended to decline in real terms, there will be added need to establish priorities under the public investment programme. This paper has argued that the current emphasis on subsidising the diffusion of mechanical technology does not amount to a considered or sensible strategy for the sector, if evaluated over the longer run. To that extent, it is likely to lead to the dissipation of public resources in a similar way to the earlier emphasis on land reclamation. Neither extensive growth nor factor substitutions can provide a strategy for agricultural growth that is either financeable or compatible with employment maximisation.

Given these limitations it is also evident that agricultural sector policy will have to go beyond shifting relative prices, whether for inputs or outputs. Raising productivity through better husbandry and the application of new agronomic packages remains a priority.

This would imply parallel improvement in the extension system; a system that is presently hardly functioning. Although Egyptian yields are high, it has been estimated that, with improved drainage and adoption of better farm practices, yields for the major cereals could be raised by around 70 per cent on average. Similar scales of increase may be possible for cotton , sugarcane, beans and lentils. For the major vegetable and fruit crops, yield increments of between 300-400 per cent may be feasible over the medium term.[20]

Complementary to direct yield increase is the issue of the intensity of production. On average, a level of 190 per cent has been attained, although in many Delta villages this has been pushed to, on or near, 200 per cent. If labour is indeed not a binding constraint, then, on the assumption of sufficient irrigation availability, such intensity levels could be raised significantly. Yet detailed studies of the irrigation system point to poor management and, in the longer run, a more constrained aggregate supply of water, as factors likely to retard this process.

Despite the fact that agriculture now generates only between 18-20 per cent of GDP and accommodates around 36 per cent of the labour force, the sector will remain critical in determining the general performance of the economy. This is likely to be enhanced in the short and medium run given the decline in external, coopted resources. While agriculture will not be able to provide self-sufficiency in food production, it is clear that a major emphasis needs to be placed on reducing the current, expanding food deficit.

This can be achieved in a number of ways. First, by reducing aggregate consumption levels of wheat products, in particular, through revisions of the subsidy system. Secondly, by restructuring the relative prices facing producers to favour food crops. At the same time, policy regarding cotton needs to be clarified. Higher producer prices are likely to elicit a strong supply response, as labour is not a critical constraint. Yet, if the present balance between exports and supplies to the domestic textile industry is maintained, this should be accompanied by greater regional specialisation and, more specifically, a shift in the mix of staples cultivated in Egypt. In other words, the area under medium or short staples should grow at the expense of long staple cotton.

The policy options pertaining to agriculture yield no easy solutions. For instance, to shift relative prices in favour of food crops and hence against livestock products would risk eliminating the foundations on which rural incomes have risen in recent years. What is clear, however, is that recent policy preferences have been largely ill-judged and in the case of the government's mechanisation strategy, based on an inaccurate evaluation of current and likely labour constraints on production.

Notes

1. C. Gotsch and W.M. Dyer, 'Rhetoric and reason in the Egyptian New Lands debate', *Food Research Institute Studies* Vol XVIII, No 2, 1982.

2. T. Tomich and C. Gotsch, *The financial and economic feasibility of reclaiming land from Egypt's northern lakes.* Discussion Paper 194, Cambridge, Mass:HIID, 1985.

3. For a fuller discussion of this issue, see Simon Commander, *The State and agricultural development in Egypt since 1973.* London, 1987.

4. See, for example, A.R. Richards and P.L. Martin, *Migration, mechanization and agricultural labour markets in Egypt.* Boulder, 1984.

5. Bent Hansen,*The Egyptian labour market.* Working Paper. Washington: World Bank, 1986.

6. See, Commander 1987.

7. A.R. Richards, *Egypt's agricultural development, 1800-1980: technical and social change.* Boulder, 1982.

8. W. Cuddihy, *Agricultural price management in Egypt.* Staff Working Paper No 388. Washington: World Bank, 1982.

9. World Bank, *Arab Republic of Egypt: issues of trade strategy and investment planning.* Washington, 1983.

10. J Von Braun and H de Haen, *The effects of food price and subsidy policies on Egyptian agriculture.* Research Report No 42, Washington: IFPRI, 1983.

11. CAPMAS, *Labour force sample survey,* 1981. Cairo, 1982.

12. A.R. Richards and P.L. Martin, 'Labour shortages in agriculture' (mimeo) Cairo, 1982.

13. Sadiq Ahmed, *Public finance in Egypt: Its structure and trends*. Staff Working Paper No 639. Washington: World Bank, 1984.

14. Commander, 1987.

15. IMF, 'Arab Republic of Egypt: recent economic developments' (mimeo), Washington, 1986.

16. World Bank, 'Egypt: Second Agricultural Development Project: staff appraisal report' (mimeo), Washington, 1985.

17. V. Levy, 'Cropping pattern, mechanization, child labour and fertility behaviour in a farming economy: rural Egypt', *Economic Development and Cultural Change*, Vol 33(4), 1985.

18. For example, N. Hopkins *et al.*, *The state of agricultural mechanization in Egypt: Results of a Survey*. Cairo: Ministry of Agriculture, 1982.

19. G.M. Scobie, *Food subsidies in Egypt: Their impact on foreign exchange and trade*. Research Report No 40, Washington: IFPRI, 1983.

20. World Bank, 1983.

7

EGYPT AND THE REGION IN THE 1980s

Charles Tripp

The legacy of Egypt's historical experience as a state has influenced its regional policies in a number of ways. This is not to say that its leaders are necessarily locked into some form of mechanical determinism, but rather that the cultural and political influences which have led to the definition of the Egyptian state have created among both rulers and ruled certain expectations regarding the role its government can shape for it in the region. The resonance of regional issues in Egyptian politics is, therefore, of prime importance. It affects attitudes towards the government's deployment of the instruments of state power, thereby raising two sorts of question. Firstly, there is the question of legitimacy, insofar as there exists a degree of common acceptance of an Egyptian national interest and of the government's right to protect and extend that interest. Secondly, there is the question of capability, relating to the perception of the resources available to the government in furthering Egypt's interests in the region. In seeking to further these interests, President Mubarak is, therefore, coming to terms with, and to a large degree acting upon the legacy he has inherited as head of the Egyptian state.

This legacy is composed of a number of elements, the first of which is the question of Egypt's identity as a national community. Although Egypt is remarkable in the Middle East in having experienced a long history as a unitary state, it has also formed the hub, and sometimes the peripheral province of far-flung

Mediterranean, Arab and Islamic empires. This has inevitably made its mark on Egypt itself, leaving much of its population with a sense that they belong not simply to Egypt, but also to larger Arab or Islamic communities. The articulation of Egyptian nationalism as a political ideal could not for long ignore these currents, and those who sought to redefine Egyptian political community with reference only to a resuscitated myth of Egypt's Pharaonic past, soon found themselves in a narrowing tributary, excluded from the mainstream of Egypt's political life. Nevertheless, it also became apparent that the attempt to submerge specifically Egyptian identity in a larger pan-Arab identity was equally impractical as a means both of advancing the interests of the state and of those who would rule the state. The mixed results of this experiment form the setting in which the present political generation has come to maturity, and constitutes, therefore, a decisive influence in their perception both of Egypt itself and of the country's proper role in the politics of the Arab world.

Equally important in the outlook of those who claim the right to rule Egypt, has been the legacy of authoritarian politics. This has led successive governments to give priority to their requirements for maintaining order within the state, and has thus led them not to question the end itself, but to concentrate on the means by which that end can be achieved. Where order becomes the supreme virtue, it suggests an overdeveloped sense of the power of the forces which threaten it and a corresponding anxiety that government should always have at its disposal the resources which will neutralise the threat. On one hand, this concerns the material resources available to the rulers: the economic and military instruments that will both feed and pacify a relentlessly growing population. On the other hand, it involves the moral resources available to the ruler, permitting him to gain common acceptance of his right to rule. In the latter respect, the identification of the President with the state is fundamental to the Egyptian system of government and demands that he find a wider regional stage on which to act out the obligations he is believed to assume in taking on the task of governing Egypt. This is a legacy which Mubarak has not simply inherited, but also consciously embraced, in that it seems to constitute an important part of his perception of executive power. This was reflected in his speech on the thirty second anniversary of the 23 July Revolution. Having dwelt at length on the importance of executive leadership, he concluded with the significant sentence 'If we distort the image of the leaders, we are actually distorting the image of the people who gave confidence to their leaders' (Cairo Home Service, BBC/SWB/ME 24 July 1984 p.1).

A further strand in the shaping of this generation, has been Egypt's experience of war. The pursuit of the interests identified as those of the Egyptian state by means of war, either against Israel or elsewhere in the Middle East, has incurred costs which have put to the test both the relationship of successive governments to the Egyptian people, and the definition of Egypt's interests which those governments proposed. The collective mobilisation and sacrifice demanded of the Egyptians in pursuit of the ends which war was intended to serve has, therefore, thrown into question the competence and the right of particular regimes to guide Egypt's destiny in the region. Failure, and the sense of disproportionate expenditure of the country's resources, contributed to the collapse of the monarchy and to the discrediting of Nasser's presidency. Sadat showed that he was aware of the danger to his own authority of launching a war which could not be directly related to the more pressing needs of Egyptian society and state. The limited war of 1973 and the peace with Israel, which was founded on that experience, were themselves the result of an accurate assessment, not only of what political society in Egypt seemed ready to tolerate, but also of what it was increasingly demanding. Mubarak and his contemporaries, as collaborators in this venture, and veterans of many of the campaigns which had preceded it , have demonstrated a corresponding caution in their approach to the use of the state's military power.

To some extent, this has been evident in handling another recurring theme in the perception of Egypt's security. Egypt's unique geography makes it a country dependent for its very survival on the river Nile. This has both consolidated its identity as a society sharing a common predicament, and has imposed upon its rulers the responsibility of ensuring that this vital resource is exploited to the maximum benefit of all. Consequently, the disposition of those who control the upper reaches of the Nile has been a constant preoccupation of Egypt's rulers, leading, at various stages in Egypt's history, to attempts to assert direct Egyptian control by force of arms. Whilst this has become impracticable in a world of sovereign states, the very size of Egypt's population has increased the urgency of ensuring that the states of the upper Nile take seriously the concern of the Egyptian government in this direction. It is a concern generated not by the changing whims and priorities of particular Egyptian leaders, but rather by the common anxiety of the collectivity as a whole, creating a collective interest that any individual leader would ignore at his peril.

This is only slightly less true in the case of the last major component of the legacy inherited by Mubarak in his dealings, on Egypt's behalf, with the outside world: the memory of Egypt's domination by external powers and their use of Egypt to serve their own interests. In this respect, the definition of Egypt's interests, the diagnosis of its ills and the claim to possess the sole remedy made by successive authorities both during the long struggle for independence and after the achievement of that independence, have been important in shaping collective attitudes towards outside powers, as well as towards the extent of legitimate government collaboration with those powers. For any government of Egypt, however, this has been tempered by the knowledge that Egypt cannot exist in isolation and, furthermore, that in order to achieve its own objectives, both domestic and regional, a considerable degree of external assistance may be required. The impression of lost independence which the soliciting and acceptance of such assistance may create has been a dilemma with which post-1952 leaders have had to grapple no less than did their predecessors under the monarchy.

These, therefore, are the main constituents of the legacy with which Mubarak must deal in shaping Egypt's role in the region in the 1980s. This is not simply a passive inheritance, but a crucial part of the way in which Mubarak and his government view the region and the rightful role of Egypt therein. It involves both the resources at its disposal and the perceived efficacy, and thus credibility -

possibly legitimacy - of the government itself. In this regard, three areas of particular concern to the government of Egypt emerge, encompassing the range of its relations with the region in which Egypt is situated. These are: firstly, Egypt's relations with Israel; secondly, Egypt's relations with the states of the Arab world in general; thirdly, Egypt's relations with its immediate neighbours in Africa - Libya and Sudan. Naturally, this will in turn lead to a consideration of the major problems facing the government of Egypt in these spheres, not simply from the perspective of domestic politics, but also with regard to the preoccupations of Egypt's principal interlocutors. The balance between suspicion of Egypt's intentions and the utility of Egypt's resources clearly determines the regional context in which Egypt can hope to play a role. Equally, the degree of success which the Egyptian government is perceived to have in exploiting this context will have significant consequences for the authority of Mubarak himself.

Egypt and Israel

In any calculation of Egypt's regional role, the relationship between Egypt and Israel must figure prominently, in the minds both of outside observers and, above all, of the Egyptian government itself. This area has been fundamental to the shaping of Egypt's identity and security, precisely because the issues it raises have a symbolic resonance which no Egyptian government can ignore. The way Egypt moves is regarded as crucial by other Arab states, which have also sought to face up to the varying levels of challenge represented by the existence of the state of Israel and by the actions of its government. For this very reason, the support of Egypt has been seen as an integral part of the effort to create a common Arab front, and the slackening of that support has been indicted as the 'betrayal' of the imagined common cause. Precisely because this has been the case, the relationship has had the capacity to impel Egyptian governments to war, in the belief that only by consecrating the resources of the state to this pan-Arab, and some would say pan-Islamic cause, could they justify their vision for Egypt's future and legitimise their own rule over the state. The catastrophic experience of war and the related belief that other means existed to secure ends which had themselves been modified by that experience, led to the Camp David process and the Washington Treaty. Consequently, the present Egyptian government must deal with three kinds of question in handling its relations with Israel.

The first of these is the very existence of the peace Treaty which underpins the current relationship. Despite the often cold relations which have existed between the Israeli and Egyptian governments, and the polemical accusations levelled by members of the former that Egypt has been in breach of the Treaty, it is not part of the Egyptian government's strategy that the Treaty should be ruptured. On the contrary, the conditions which necessitated its signature in 1979 remain no less present in the 1980s. When Butros Butros-Ghali stated that Egypt was 'pursuing peace not out of altruism, but out of necessity' (Interview in *Les Cahiers de l'Orient* 1986/2 p.64), he was referring to the regional and domestic dangers with which the government of Egypt would have to cope, were there no peace Treaty in existence.

On one hand, Egypt would be faced by the possibility of war with Israel. This would be even more likely to occur if any Egyptian government decided suddenly to abrogate the Treaty, since the fears it would arouse in Israel would be certain to provoke a military response. On the other hand, in the absence of a peace Treaty, Egypt would be the recipient neither of external military and civilian aid on the scale currently enjoyed, nor of the investment which it has sought to encourage. Equally, there would be the threatened loss of the Suez Canal dues and of the revenues from the Sinai oilfields. Whilst the present government of Egypt may have fewer illusions than Sadat about the nature of the economic benefits flowing from adherence to the Treaty, there is, nevertheless, a recognition that it remains fundamental to the way Egypt is to be governed. The military relationship with the USA is important to the powerful military faction within the government, allowing it not only to reinforce its preponderant influence in the shaping of national policy, but also to reorganise the Egyptian armed forces along the lines believed most suited to securing its position as the major instrument of the projection of Egypt's power. In the words of Butros Butros-Ghali, 'We need the peace process to solve our internal problems.....therefore we have the will to continue' (*International Herald Tribune* 24 February 1984).

The alternatives are such that staying with the Treaty itself, however unsatisfactory the process may seem at times, is indeed a necessity for Mubarak. It allows him to placate the military and to call upon the massive external resources needed to sustain Egypt's population above a dangerous level of destitution. Nor are there many significant pressures within the state for an abrogation of the Treaty. Those who participate publicly in politics and who claim to support the government must perforce subscribe to the Treaty itself. This does not ensure wholehearted acquiescence, let alone enthusiasm. For those in opposition, there is the problem of how they would foresee the course of future relations with Israel. There is also, of course, the question of the degree of influence they can realistically expect or exert on the government over a question of national security. A number of those who advocate a complete rupture with Israel are also those whose other political prescriptions demonstrate a certain failure to think through the practical consequences of their advocacy. They are, as a consequence, confined to the fringes of Egyptian politics, meriting little attention from the government, except when their activities seem to threaten public order.

Acceptance of the Washington Treaty as the basic framework for relations between Egypt and Israel is, therefore, likely to remain a vital part of the definition of Egypt's regional role. Nevertheless, it begs the second major question which the Mubarak government must face. This concerns the ways in which Egyptian-Israeli relations can best be conducted within that framework. Clearly, Mubarak did not intend that it should be used by Israel to imply Egyptian acquiescence in Israel's regional activities. Whatever the benefits of the Treaty, this would have been unacceptable to any Egyptian government, not least because many of the policies pursued by Israel in the region and within the territories occupied in 1967, have caused consternation across a wide spectrum of political opinion in Egypt itself. For Mubarak to have given the impression of condoning such activities would have been to erode his own authority, not simply among those who reject the very idea of peaceful relations with Israel, but, more significantly, among those who depend upon him to manage successfully these unruly constituencies.

Maintaining relations on an equable footing has, therefore, largely depended upon the nature and proclivities of the Israeli government of the day. The Israeli invasion of Lebanon in 1982, and its aftermath, led to a virtual suspension of relations between Egypt and Israel for these very reasons. In June of that year, much of the opposition in Egypt had called for a rupture of relations because of the invasion itself. The Egyptian government resisted such calls, but responded by breaking off the desultory talks on Palestinianautonomy and by reducing economic and cultural exchanges. However, following the massacres at Sabra and Shattila camps in September, with their intensely emotive impact, the Egyptian government recalled its ambassador to Israel and initiated an effective freeze on further official contacts between the two countries. Although some talks of a minor nature were restarted in spring of 1983, the coming to power of Shamir as Prime Minister was clearly discouraging for the Egyptians.(Kramer 1983 p.642) For his part, he accused Egypt of reneging on the Treaty because of the refusal of the Egyptian government to restart talks on Palestinian autonomy. The Egyptian government responded by stating that normal relations between the two countries could not exist whilst Israel pursued its current regional policy, citing such events as the 1981 bombing of the Iraqi nuclear reactor, the 1982 invasion of Lebanon and the nature of Israel's policies on the West Bank and in Gaza as the real obstacles to normalisation. (*Guardian* 12 October 1983)

In such circumstances, and while the Likud government remained in office, there seemed to be few prospects for any significant progress in relations between the two countries. By the end of 1983, specific negotiations were confined to discussions about the future of the enclave at Taba and the status of several thousand Palestinians at Rafah camp who had found themselves excluded from the Gaza strip, following the return of Sinai to Egyptian sovereignty in 1982. However, since these were conducted against a background of mutual suspicion, little headway was made. (*Times* 11 November 1983) It was only with the coming to power of the National Unity government after the Israeli elections of 1984 that a certain thaw in relations began to set in. Mubarak saw in the dilution of Likud influence within that government the possibility of Israel meeting the three conditions which he had publicly defined in 1984 as constituting the prerequisites for the resumption of normal relations. These were, firstly, the withdrawal of Israeli forces from Lebanon, secondly, the achievement of significant progress on the Taba issue, and lastly, movement towards the resolution of the 'Palestinian problem'.(BBC/SWB/ME 31 July 1984 p.1) In the absence of any such progress, relations between Israel and Egypt, despite hopes raised by the signing of the Treaty, seemed likely to remain 'an armistice which is working well, with a few economic and other contacts'.(*Times* 27 March 1984)

With Peres as Prime Minister of Israel, the Egyptian government was clearly more optimistic that its conditions could be met. The withdrawal from Lebanon, even though hedged around with measures that implied a continuing Israeli capacity and intention to intervene, was in the process of being carried out. This was, of course, due to the changing situation in Lebanon, the increasing cost of the Israeli presence in that country, and to Peres' own conviction that the whole venture had been unwise. His Likud partners were in no position to object, given the outcome of the Lebanon experience. On the Taba issue, however, the Egyptian government could be considerably more active. During 1985 and 1986 this became one of the major points of contact between the Israeli and Egyptian governments. Reassuringly for the Egyptian government, it became a technical dispute over the most acceptable means of adjudicating the future status of this small area of the Sinai coast, conducted impeccably within the framework of the Treaty. The advantages for the Egyptian government were numerous. It was a concrete case of border demarcation, such as might arise between any two contiguous states. In focusing upon it, therefore, the very normality of Egyptian-Israeli relations was underlined. This, after all, was one of the chief intentions of the sponsors of the Treaty.(Harkabi 1986 pp.2-4) In addition, precisely because the territory involved raised none of the contentious socio-political and ideological issues raised by the future of other territories occupied by Israel, there was a strong possibility that the Egyptian government would win their argument that the matter should be settled by international arbitration. A 'victory' in this sense would cause no damage to the relationship between the two states, but it would redound to the credit of Mubarak, both regionally and domestically. This, in turn, might make him more confident in tackling the far more thorny and important question of the future of the Palestinians, which the dispute over Taba had succeeded, providentially, in obscuring.

Peres and his Labour colleagues in the government appeared to be convinced of the utility of this issue in the senses outlined above, and were willing to concede the Egyptian demand for international arbitration, in order to address the larger questions between the two countries. However, they were met by opposition from the Likud bloc, which wanted to submit the matter to a process of non-binding conciliation, in the hope perhaps that this would give Israel a short-term advantage, as well as delay the negotiations on the future of the Palestinians.(*Times* 18 May 1985; *Guardian* 19 June 1985) During 1986, the Taba dispute became, in many respects, a matter of internal Israeli politics, as Peres sought to persuade Shamir of the importance of accepting the Egyptian demand for international arbitration. After considerable pressure from Peres, which reportedly included a threat to bring down the government itself, Shamir and the Likud bloc agreed and paved the way for the agreement between Egypt and Israel of September 1986 to submit the matter to international arbitration.(*Times* 14 January 1986; *Financial Times* 12 August 1986; *Guardian* 11 September 1986)

The resolution of this issue in the sense agreed upon was a gain for Mubarak's government. It had stood by its original position and forcefully argued its case over a period of two years. In many important ways, the agreement could be portrayed not only as a success for Egypt, but also for Mubarak's leadership. It was thus very much the kind of issue needed by the *rayyis* to reinforce his authority. It was perhaps disproportionately important, simply because there were few other instances of marked success in other areas of the relationship. The settlement of the question of arbitration allowed Mubarak to hold a summit meeting with Peres (the first between the leaders of the two countries since the death of Sadat), to upgrade Egypt's representation in Israel to ambassadorial status and to turn his attention to the third major question which arises between Egypt and Israel: the future of the Palestinians.(BBC/SWB/ME 13 September 1986 pp.1-4)

The question of the Palestinians and of their future political status must inevitably hang over the Egyptian-Israeli relationship. Israel was established at the expense of the intended Arab state of Palestine. It was the rejection of the legitimacy of this venture, together with feelings of solidarity throughout the Middle East with a fellow Muslim and Arab community, which made it impossible for the government of Egypt to ignore the Palestinians, leading to its engagement in the central Arab-Israeli conflict. The experience of that conflict may have resulted in a determination to seek a solution by peaceful means rather than by war, but it did not mean that the Egyptian government had renounced its concern. The Camp David agreements, and the Treaty that followed, were indicted by the majority of Arab states as a betrayal of the Palestinians, since their future was subordinated to the immediate requirements of the Egyptian state.

Whilst it is undoubtedly true - and scarcely surprising - that Egyptian priorities formed the impetus and main basis of the Treaty, nevertheless these very concerns could not be wholly divorced from concern for the Palestinians. However exasperated Sadat may have been with the Palestinian leadership, and however little patience he may have felt for specifically Palestinian interests when set against those of Egypt, he was aware that it would have been politically foolhardy to have explicitly abandoned their cause. This explains the second part of the Camp David agreements, referring to the question of Palestinian autonomy, as well as his constant use of the argument that the Treaty was simply the first stage on the path of a comprehensive settlement of all outstanding issues between Israel and the Arabs.

In the event, Sadat did not live to see the completion of the first part of the Camp David accords, and his commitment to negotiating a solution to the problem of the Palestinians was therefore never put to the test, becoming instead the subject of a good deal of polemical conjecture. For Mubarak, however, it was important that he should turn his attention to this issue, following the return of the whole of the Sinai peninsula to Egypt in 1982. Firstly, it would serve as proof of the continuity with the policies of his predecessor which he had pledged himself to follow. It was, therefore, an important element in cementing the allegiance of the political class in Egypt around his person. Secondly, by focusing on the area which the Egyptian government had long been accused of neglecting, he would both be vindicating those policies and seizing the opportunity to create for himself a wider constituency of support within Egypt and the region than had been available to Sadat. This, in turn, reinforced his own claim to rule the Egyptian state. At the same time, however, Mubarak was responding to, or perhaps merely voicing, a widespread feeling in Egypt that peace between Egypt and Israel would only be fully realisable and stable under the conditions of a comprehensive settlement of the issues dividing Israel and the Arab world in general. Clearly it would be to Egypt's advantage, and to that of its President, if Egypt were to be instrumental in brokering such a dramatic development in the Middle East. Equally, in the absence of such a settlement, there was the realisation that the Treaty can be merely a form of armistice. Evidence of this was amply provided following the suspension of all talks on Palestinian autonomy as a result of the Israeli government's attempt to impose its desired solution on the Palestinians in 1982.

Subsequently, Mubarak has been active in the advocacy of any framework for the solution of the Palestinian issue which might enlist the support of others, be they international organisations or particular states, for the idea that a settlement must take into account the Palestinians' desire for self-determination. This is due to the realisation, on Egypt's part, that the nature of the issue is such that Egypt is ill-placed to succeed in convincing the Israeli government in bilateral negotiations that the Palestinians should be granted the measure of autonomy which alone would satisfy them.

Mubarak's own experience in this respect, as well as that of his predecessor, has convinced him that Egypt and Israel bring to such negotiations not only very different conceptions of the ultimate political status of the Palestinians, but also very different kinds of determination to ensure that those conceptions are realised. For any Israeli government, the ultimate decision on this issue raises questions about the future political constitution and security of Israel as a state. For the Egyptian government, however resonant the Palestinian cause may be within Egyptian politics, the fate of the Palestinians is a less pressing concern than the fate of the Egyptians themselves. This sense of differing priorities was underlined when Mubarak remarked that despite the intensemedia coverage of Egypt's involvement in foreign policy questions, 90 per cent of his time was taken up in attending to domestic matters.(*Times* 10 December 1984) This may be somewhat disengenuous, given the degree to which Egyptian governments are tempted to use foreign policy questions as a means of disguising the gravity of domestic crises. However, there is an element of truth in this remark. It indicates the relatively reduced determination - not unrelated to capacity - which the Egyptian government can bring to negotiation with Israel over an important, but nevertheless secondary issue.

As a result, during the past few years, Mubarak has been keen to encourage any moves that might bring Israel to negotiate the future of the Palestinians, in a forum which might face Israel with more formidable interlocutors than Egypt alone. To this end, Egypt, together with France, put to the U.N. Security Council a proposal that called for the mutual recognition of Israel and the PLO as a preliminary move to direct negotiations. In November 1982, encouraged by the Reagan Plan and by the Fez summit resolutions, Mubarak presented his seven point plan calling for direct negotiations between Israel and the PLO on the basis of these proposals. In an attempt to begin the induction of the PLO into the peace process, Mubarak gave an official welcome to Yasser Arafat as he passed through the Suez Canal after his expulsion from Lebanon in 1983. The hope, evidently, was that the PLO might moderate its stance, thereby engaging the interest of the United States in starting a dialogue with the only authoritative representative of the Palestinians.(*Financial Times* 23 December

1983; BBC/SWB/ME 23 December 1983 pp.6-7) Indeed, the efforts exerted by Mubarak during this period seem to testify to his belief that two vital components were required for any comprehensive peace process to succeed: firstly, the United States which, although the ally of Israel, remained the only power which could realistically be expected to exert leverage in Israeli politics; secondly, the PLO, without whose participation no peace settlement could be expected to gain acceptance, either among the generality of the Palestinians themselves, or among the Arab states. He envisaged Egypt's role, therefore, as being that of an active mediator which could bring these elements together into a negotiating framework.

To this end, Mubarak sought to promote the idea of a Jordanian-Palestinian federation and joint negotiating team favoured by the US administration. In 1984 he visited a number of European states, seeking European support for the idea of a wider peace conference. In 1985, Egyptian officials claimed that Mubarak was instrumental in persuading Jordan and the PLO to sign the agreement of February that year which seemed to presage a serious attempt to bring the PLO into the peace process. Equally, on his March 1985 visit to Washington, Mubarak tried to persuade the US administration of the desirability of dealing directly with Jordan and the PLO as a preliminary to a peace conference with Israeli participation.(*I.H.T.* 15/16 June 1985) However, although he was determined to further this process, there were clearly limitations on Egypt's capacity, single-handedly, to do so. With the rupture in Jordanian-PLO relations in 1986, the Egyptian government was forced to acknowledge that it had limited influence in this direction, and equally little influence with the US administration.(Shamir 1986 pp.188-189 ; *Financial Times* 4 June 1986)

Nevertheless, it is clearly important for Mubarak to be seen to be active in this respect. It was significant that, following his return from his visit of European capitals, he is reported to have remarked that he was satisfied to have been treated as a leader for the first time in his own right.(*Times* 10 December 1984) It was, therefore, scarcely suprising that he should have become an early and enthusiastic advocate of the idea of an international conference as the proper forum for the negotiation and settlement of issues at stake between Israel and the Arabs, regardless perhaps of its very uncertain outcome. The convening of such a conference would represent a legitimation of Egypt's role and of the part it had been playing in regional affairs. None of this would be lost on Mubarak's internal constituencies.

However, quite apart from these considerations, Mubarak evidently sees it as perhaps the only means of overcoming the intractability of Israeli politics, and the resistance the latter represents to the idea of Palestinian self-determination. Before the advent of the National Unity government, it was clear that there could be no common ground between the Egyptian and the Israeli governments over the preconditions for negotiation regarding the Palestinians, nor over the ultimate objective of such negotiations.(Mubarak interview, *U.S. News and World Report* 14 January 1985) With Peres as Prime Minister, albeit of a coalition government, there was greater optimism in Egypt that some moderation of the Israeli rejection of an international conference might take place. As far as Peres was concerned, this was indeed the case and, to the annoyance of his Likud Cabinet colleagues, he seemed increasingly to endorse the idea, without however accepting the Egyptian proposal of PLO participation. This allowed Mubarak and Peres to declare at their September 1986 summit that 1987 would be 'the year of peace negotiations', during which they would concentrate their efforts on reviving a comprehensive peace process.(*Ruz al-Yusuf* 15 September 1986 pp.3-5)

In December 1986 Mubarak was to claim that Egypt was attempting to reconcile the PLO and Jordan, that an international peace conference was a real possibility and that he found much ground for encouragement in Peres' attitude. However, at the same time, he expressed grave misgivings about the inflexibility and policies of Shamir who was on the verge of taking over as Prime Minister in Israel.(*Le Monde* 10 December 1986) Subsequent events appear to have justified his pessimism. Despite threatening to bring down the government and to force a general election on the very issue of an international peace conference and the future of the occupied territories, Peres backed down from going to such lengths, uncertain of the support he could find in Israel. Reconciliation between Jordan and the PLO seemed as far away as ever, particularly after the Palestine National Council meeting in Algiers. Nor did there seem to be much purpose to such a reconciliation as long as US policy in the Middle East remained paralysed by uncertainty and confusion.

With the launching of the 'Shultz initiative' in early 1988, Mubarak clearly found some grounds for hope. In the first place, it seemed to represent an American commitment to the idea of an international conference as the best means of resolving the Arab-Israeli conflict. This had been a view long held by Mubarak. Secondly, American advocacy of some form of immediate local autonomy for the Palestinians of the West Bank and Gaza was a welcome attempt to put life into the moribund 'Camp David Part 2'. Lastly, the very evident reluctance of Prime Minister Shamir to become engaged in the process would, it was hoped, convince the United States government of the obduracy of any Likud dominated government in Israel. In that respect, it would reinforce the Egyptian contention that this inflexibility on the part of Israel was the real obstacle to a comprehensive peace. It was, therefore, logical that Mubarak should give Secretary of State Shultz every encouragement on the latter's visit to Egypt at the beginning of March 1988. However, it also became clear that, although the United States government was undoubtedly cheered by the Egyptian endorsement of its proposals, the crucial consideration was whether Israel, on one side, and the PLO, on the other, would agree to the idea of negotiations within such a framework.

In these circumstances, Mubarak could scarcely hope that Egypt's voice would make a very great impression. In its dealings with Israel, therefore, over this central question of the Palestinians - a question which must eventually decide the nature of the Egyptian-Israeli relationship itself - Mubarak has discovered the limits to Egyptian influence. Frustration of this nature is unsettling for any authoritarian ruler. For an Egyptian President, helplessness in this particular setting might also dangerously erode his own authority, since it prevents him from allaying the criticisms levelled against the Egyptian government on this emotive issue from various sectors of Egyptian political society. More importantly, it makes him look like a passive victim of trends in regional politics, confined to reacting merely to the initiatives of others. This accords neither with the expectations vested in the power of the *rayyis,* nor, through him, with Egyptians' expectations of the rightful role of their country in the world.

Egypt and the Arab World

Frustration in this direction has been matched by the equal intractability of inter-Arab politics to Egyptian direction. In 1984, a senior Egyptian official remarked that 'We have our objective: we want peace and we want to rebuild our country. But try to give me the objective of any other country in the area, and I will tell you they do not know what they want. It is like dealing with ghosts.'(*I.H.T.* 24 February 1984) In essence, this statement captures two of the major themes in Egypt's dealings with the Arab world. The first is the sense of Egypt's own pre-eminence. The second is frustration at the inability of the Egyptian government to gain sufficient acknowledgement of that leading role to allow Egypt to set the agenda for the Arab world as a whole, especially regarding a settlement of the Arab-Israeli issue.

As far as the first theme is concerned, the belief that, whatever happens, Egypt will remain the primary Arab state, is founded on the very historical and political legacies which have shaped Egyptians' views of themselves and of their state. This has given the Egyptian government relative confidence in its dealings with the fleeting internal and regional coalitions of Arab politics. At the height of Nasser's conviction of his own and his country's regional mission, this was transformed into an overweening determination to reorder the internal politics of other Arab states and to construct regional blocs and alliances more to the liking of the Egyptian President. Despite a certain nostalgia among some circles in Egypt for the illusion of power which this created, such an interventionist policy in the region has been tempered by the experience of the costs of attempting to sustain it. The Egyptian government has, therefore, been obliged to come to terms with Egypt's reduced capacities in this regard. However, the idea that Egypt need not defer to others in the region and that, as Mubarak said, 'Egypt will remain the leading state in this region, whether the others like it or not', remains an important part of the perception of rulers and ruled alike.(*I.H.T.* 14 February 1984)

It is, therefore, equally important that the Egyptian President should be seen to define and protect this role. This means neither denying Egypt an active role in the Arab world, nor allowing that role to become a subordinate one in which Egypt must perforce follow the dictates of others. Mubarak inherited a Treaty with Israel in the utility of which he firmly believes, but he also inherited the isolation of Egypt from much of the Arab world, caused by Arab reactions to the signature of that Treaty. One of the persistent themes of his regional policy has, therefore, been the effort to improve ties between Egypt and the Arab states, but on the firm understanding that such an improvement would not be at the expense of Israeli-Egyptian relations. In doing so, he has discovered to his gratification, and to the confirmation of many Egyptian views about the nature of their fellow Arab states, that it does indeed seem as if the Arab world cannot, in fact, do without Egypt.

The 'isolation' instituted after the Baghdad summits had in reality been less total than the word might suggest. The breaking off of diplomatic relations, the expulsion of Egypt from the Arab League and from the Islamic Conference Organisation, and the suspension of other state-to-state contacts had had considerable symbolic resonance. However, they had not prevented either the human or cultural resources of Egypt from maintaining their predominance in the Arab world. Nor had they altered the perception of Egypt itself as a force for stability in the troubled politics of the area. Indeed, the combination of this perception and the parlous state of the Arab world during the 1980s have worked to Egypt's and thus to Mubarak's advantage. A number of states re-established close formal and informal relations with Egypt, encouraged by Egypt's own initiatives but also acting upon their own perception of the aid which Egypt's support can give to their own particular projects.

Morocco and Jordan, were to re-establish diplomatic relations with Egypt in 1984. This had been preceded by the re-admission of Egypt to the I.C.O. in January of that year and by meetings between Mubarak and the leaders of the two states. The King of Morocco had been an unconvinced signatory to the Baghdad summit resolutions. He, himself, had few inhibitions about contacts with the Israeli government, as his reception of Prime Minister Peres in Morocco in 1986 was to demonstrate. Equally, he saw considerable utility in contacts between Egypt and Morocco, since he needed allies in his continuing claim to the Western Sahara, enjoyed a similarly close relationship with the US and shared many of the perceptions of the Egyptian government about the threats to the security of the region. King Hussein of Jordan, caught between the Arab-Israeli conflict on one side and the Iran-Iraq war on the other, was equally in need of the support which an alliance with Egypt might grant. On the former, Egyptian support to some extent offset Syrian hostility in Jordan's attempt to persuade the PLO of the need to negotiate, in the preliminary stages at least, with a view to creating a Palestinian-Jordanian federation. It was also thought valuable to have an Egyptian voice added to that of Jordan when seeking to persuade the United States to take an active role in setting up a framework for negotiation with Israel. As far as the Iran-Iraq war was concerned, the seriousness of Iraq's plight meant that King Hussein could only look with relief on the aid which Egypt was able to give to the government in Baghdad.

The war has, in fact, been instrumental in allowing a large number of Arab states to re-establish formal relations with Egypt. In the forefront has been Iraq itself. In its effort to draw on the resources of the region to sustain Iraq's defence, the Iraqi government has made use of Egypt's armaments industry and its military expertise. Egyptian arms and ammunition exports to Iraq have amounted to roughly $3,000 million and a number of Egyptian army officers have been freed to serve in the Iraqi armed forces. The latter have also been reinforced by several units formed from the very large Egyptian community living in Iraq. There have been many exchanges of visits between officials of the two countries, including a visit to Iraq by President Mubarak at a moment of crisis in the fighting.(Tripp 1986 pp.502-3; King 1987 pp.42-43)

In 1985 Taha Ramadhan suggested that the restoration of diplomatic relations with Egypt, while the Treaty with Israel remained in force, was still too difficult a step for an Iraqi government concerned with its own domestic security and its position in the region. Nevertheless, it was noticeable that the Iraqi position on the role of the Palestinians and on the question of the recognition of, and even negotiation with Israel was moving markedly closer to that of Egypt.(Taha Ramadhan interview with Al-Majalis, quoted in BBC/SWB/ME 16 July 1985 p.6; Saddam Hussein interview of 25 August 1982, in BBC/SWB/ME 5 January 1983 p.6) These were encouraging trends for the Egyptian government. They tended to bear out the thesis that Egypt's human and military resources and regional weight would count for more in the long run, and in the parlous state of Arab politics, than mere financial power or claimed ideological purity. In November 1987, at the Arab Summit in Amman, Egypt received unequivocal confirmation of this fact. It was then, at a Summit called to discuss the threat of the war with Iran to the Arab world as a whole, that Iraq abandoned its earlier inhibitions and strongly advocated the full and unconditional 'rehabilitation' of Egypt. Although this was insufficient to cause Egypt's re-admission to the Arab League, it did nevertheless lead to the restoration of full and formal diplomatic relations between Egypt and the great majority of Arab states, led by Iraq.

Encouraging and reinforcing as this may be for Mubarak, it is nevertheless noticeable that he has experienced considerable frustration in attempting to exploit this fact of Egypt's relative strength to increase its capacity to influence regional developments. The difficulty of transforming Egypt's many links with the Arab world into a durable coalition that might indeed accept Egypt's leadership, and particularly its direction towards a comprehensive settlement with Israel, has been a marked feature of the past few years. Nor is it likely to change radically in the foreseeable future. On the one hand, this constitutes an obstacle to the implementation of a regional vision which the Egyptian government believes will best secure its interests. On the other hand, power can only be effective when it is acknowledged to be so, and the failure of Mubarak to use Egypt's apparent assets to secure such acknowledgement inevitably raises the question about his competence - and possible right - to be trustee of Egypt's interests.

These elements have been most marked in Egypt's relationship with the PLO. Mubarak has declared that Egypt has no right to negotiate on the Palestinian question independently and, furthermore, any attempt to do so without authoritative Palestinian approval would simply be made unworkable through rejection by the Palestinians themselves.(Mubarak interview, *U.S. News and World Report* 14 January 1985) The problem has been, as ever, finding representatives of the Palestinians who would not only be willing to negotiate, but would also have sufficient authority to ensure acceptance of the outcome of the negotiations. In the post-Beirut phase of the PLO's existence there was evidently some optimism that the misfortune which had recently befallen the organisation would lead to a significant change of strategy, despite Mubarak's misgivings about the notorious insecurity and thus vacillation of its leadership.(Mubarak interview, *Guardian* 18 January 1983) Nevertheless, the thrust of Egyptian policy was to encourage the PLO under Arafat's leadership to enter into an agreement with Jordan which might eventually lead to negotiations with the US and possibly with Israel.

During 1985 and 1986, however, it became clear that the factors preventing the PLO from accepting the preconditions which would make it an acceptable interlocutor for the US, were as insuperable as ever. They were not amenable to Egyptian persuasion, despite the best efforts of Mubarak, and they led eventually to the rupture between Jordan and the PLO in February 1986.(Shamir 1986 p.189) Faced with the collapse of the hoped for coalition that would carry the peace process forward in the sense desired by Egypt, the Egyptian government could only hope that not all was lost, but it was clearly unable to do anything to justify that optimism. (*Financial Times* 4 June 1986) The internal workings of the PLO, a re-emerging traditional rivalry between Egypt and Syria in the Levant, as well as the attitudes of the US and of Israel, combined to thwart the Egyptian government's intentions in this sphere.

Although frustrated on this front and unable to profit, therefore, from the use of Egypt's power in a sense that might enhance its regional role, Mubarak was determined that the PLO - and possibly also his internal Egyptian constituency - should appreciate the cost involved in the rejection of Egyptian guidance. The meeting of the Palestine National Council in Algiers in April 1987 provided him with the opportunity of stressing this fact. The explicit warning given to the leadership of the PLO prior to the passing of the resolutions that were intended to secure internal unity, at the expense of relations with Jordan and Egypt, and the subsequent action taken against PLO representatives in Egypt, were a demonstration that Egypt could not be lightly spurned. The harshness of the Egyptian reaction may well have been an expression of the disappointment felt by Egyptian officials that, once again, the Palestinian leadership was 'politicking by realigning themselves, but at the expense of a rational Palestinian strategy'.(*Financial Times* 27 April 1987; *I.H.T.* 28 April 1987) However, it also seems to have been due to the need for Mubarak to show his own countrymen, as well as others in the region, that Egypt was a power that must be taken seriously. The failure of the PNC to heed the Egyptian warning, of course, demonstrated that the Palestinians were not convinced of the centrality of Egypt to their future strategy. This is something of an embarrassment, since it accords neither with the Egyptian government's, nor with the opposition's view about what Egypt's role is and ought to be.

Egypt and its African Neighbours

In its relations with Libya and Sudan, the Egyptian government has needed to exercise considerable restraint, born of the realisation that although political developments within these two countries have the capacity to affect Egyptian security, the Egyptian government itself has few means of influencing the course of those developments. As far as Libya is concerned, this has led to a policy of considered inaction, accompanied by the use of explicit warnings and by the deployment of the resources of the Egyptian state to deter any hostile initiative from the Libyan government. In the case of Sudan, the major preoccupation of the Egyptian government has been that the ferment of Sudanese politics should not produce a regime intrinsically hostile to Egyptian interests, nor over-receptive to regional forces which might themselves be hostile to Egypt. Although contacts with Sudan are considerably more extensive than those with Libya, the scale of the political problems affecting Sudan is such that Egypt can only play a minor role in encouraging their solution.

In Qadhafi of Libya, the Egyptian government has had to face the animosity of a leader who believed that Egypt would provide him with the vehicle for preponderant influence in the Arab world and who consequently felt cheated when the actual inheritors of Nasser's state refused to recognise his claim to be Nasser's true heir.   This led, inevitably, to a sharp deterioration in relations between the two states, sustained by Qadhafi's conviction of his own rectitude and by the Egyptian government's rejection of the demands made upon it. The dispute ranged initially over issues of regional concern, specifically regarding the policies pursued by Egypt towards the Arab-Israeli conflict and towards the Arab world in general. However, in the face of the lack of response and indeed rejection with which Qadhafi met, he came to the conclusion that the government of Egypt was illegitimate and that it was in the process of betraying the true interests of the Egyptian people, for whom he himself claimed to speak. On one level, this led to a campaign of rhetorical recrimination and vilification, into which Sadat entered with gusto. On another level, it led to Libyan dabbling in the activities of the fringe groups of the Egyptian political underworld, who shared with Qadhafi the delusion that their occasional acts of violence would have disproportionately dramatic consequences in Egyptian politics.(*Le Monde* 8 February 1977 and 1 June 1977)

When Mubarak came to power he showed himself less inclined to indulge in the form of propaganda war whichSadat had relished. For his part, Qadhafi hoped that the death of his sworn enemy Sadat would provide new openings and new receptiveness to his ambitions in Egypt. In this he was to be disappointed. Relations between the two countries returned to the level of previous years, although, for connoisseurs of the genre, the insults exchanged lacked the true inventiveness of the preceding era. As far as the material expression of this enmity was concerned, the Egyptian government continued to be wary in two respects. Firstly, there was continuing concern in Egypt about the degree of aid Qadhafi might be giving to a number of subversive organisations within Egypt. In general, the deployment of the considerable internal security apparatus of the Egyptian state was sufficient to thwart any Libyan designs. Secondly, there was the propensity of Qadhafi to give shelter and some support to small Palestinian groups who believed that violent tactics in the region could have a disproportionately large effect on the peace process. During 1985 and 1986, the fragility of that process did, indeed, seem to be emphasised by a number of such incidents, including the hijacking of an Egyptian aircraft to Malta with disastrous consequences. Possibly as a means of diverting attention from the mistakes made by the Egyptian commandos in storming the plane, Mubarak made his strongest verbal attack to date against Libya. Blaming Qadhafi for having been ultimately responsible for the incident, he promised a 'severe' reply, placed Egypt's air defence command on the alert and intiated a series of military manoeuvres along the Libyan border.(*Guardian* 27 November 1985 and 2 December 1985)

Unlike his predecessor, however, Mubarak has shown marked reluctance to become involved militarily against Libya. Undoubtedly aware of the repercussions inside the Egyptian armed forces of the brief border war of 1977, as well as of the wider regional resonance of using Egypt's armed forces against another Arab state, it was scarcely surprising that Mubarak was reported to have rejected US proposals of joint military action in 1985/86.(*Guardian* 1 April 1986; *I.H.T.* 3 April 1986) The costs of such action at a number of levels, quite apart from the uncertainty of the outcome, have made it an unattractive option for Mubarak. Libyan animosity has hurt Egyptian interests - most severely perhaps in the expulsion of 100,000 Egyptian workers during 1985 (*Times* 24 August 1985) - but not to a degree that would justify military action. In most respects, therefore, Libya is a country which Mubarak can effectively freeze out of its regional calculations until such time as a change of heart occurs within the Libyan regime itself.

The case of Sudan, however, is rather different. Its very situation, astride the upper reaches of the Nile, makes its security and the attitude of its government a matter of vital of importance to the Egyptian government. Prior to his overthrow in April 1985, Nimayri had been a far from reassuring ally for Egypt. Despite his proclaimed friendship, he was politically isolated within the country and had been largely responsible for provoking the renewed outbreak of civil war in the South. Egypt had felt the effect of this war almost at once in the abrupt ending of further work on the Jonglei Canal scheme in 1983. Subsequently, the Egyptian government has been concerned on two counts: firstly, that the new regime in Khartoum should continue to bear in mind Egypt's own security requirements in its endeavours to repair Sudan's regional relations, especially with Libya; secondly, that the civil war in the South should be brought to an end.

As far as the first element is concerned, the transitional military government in Sudan, which ruled the country following the overthrow of Nimayri, alarmed the Egyptian government by showing itself highly receptive to Qadhafi's overtures and by concluding a military agreement with Libya. However, General Sawar al-Dhahab succeeded in allaying Egyptian fears to some degree, by pointing out that the rapprochement with Libya was largely aimed at ending Libyan support for the SPLA in the South. Equally, it was made clear to the Egyptian government that the military agreement signed with Libya was not to be at the expense of the rather more extensive security agreement that already existed between Egypt and Sudan. (*Guardian* 9 May 1985; *Le Monde* 27 August 1985 and 31 October 1985)

With the succession of a civilian government in Sudan under Sadiq al-Mahdi as Prime Minister, a number of minor issues arose to trouble relations between the two states. In reality, these testified to a lingering distrust on both sides. The Sudanese government was suspicious of the fact that Nimayri remained in Egypt, whilst the Egyptian government was not wholly reassured about the vulnerability of the impoverished Sudanese administration to the blandishments of Libya. Nevertheless, after a period marked by rather cool relations between Egypt and Sudan, the traditional relationship could be seen to re-emerge during 1986/87. The Sudanese Prime Minister visited Egypt in 1987 and took the opportunity to sign the 'Brotherhood Charter' amidst general expressions of goodwill. Significantly enough, his visit also included tours of Egyptian munitions factories and lengthy conversations with the Egyptian Minister of Defence.(*Sudanow* May 1987 p.29; *Le Monde* 24 February 1987)

This was, of course, relevant to the other area of Egyptian concern: the ending of the civil war. The Egyptian government has been willing to provide the Sudanese government with a certain amount of military assistance, in terms of arms, ammunition and, possibly, advisers. The intention is to enable the hard-pressed Sudanese armed forces at least to hold their own against the attacks of the SPLA in the southern provinces. Insofar as can be judged, this assistance seems to have had some effect. At the same time, the Egyptian government has sought to act as an intermediary between the Sudanese and the Ethiopian governments, in an effort to persuade the latter to curb the activities of the SPLA operating from Ethiopian territory. This has had mixed results. Whilst Egyptian efforts seem to be continuing, both on its own account and on that of the Sudanese government, the fact remains that a solution to the civil war in Sudan must arise from specifically Sudanese developments that are largely unamenable to significant Egyptian influence.

Conclusion

Egypt remains one of the major powers in the region. The vigour of its cultural life and the ubiquity of its influence make it a force which cannot be ignored in the Arab world. At the same time, the instruments of state power in the hands of its rulers and the comparative confidence with which they handle power itself, make it a formidable state in a region of shifting political identity and allegiance. Even the very scale of its difficulties, both economic and demographic, give some indication of the relative magnitude of Egypt compared to its neighbours. The problem has been to exploit the given weight of Egypt in order to secure the perceived interests of the state. This, in turn, raises questions about the identity of the state itself, and therefore about the nature of its best interests in the region. Some of these questions remain crucially unresolved, despite the relative stability of Egyptian politics and the degree, as well as location of the consensus on which that stability is founded. Even on the basis of minimum agreement among the constituencies that matter, there remains the problem of matching the human and financial resources at the disposal of Egypt's ruler to the task he has set himself. By the 1980s this task has been shorn of most of its earlier ideological pretensions, becoming rather a process of pragmatic adjustment. It is informed, however, by a concern to preserve the authority of the President himself through his successful representation of Egypt and visible extension of its interests, since this seems to many to be the sole guarantee of order.

In the three areas of regional concern discussed above, the Egyptian government appears to want others to make compromises as great as those which it believes itself to have made with regard both to what it should do and what it can do in the region. However, given the state of regional politics and of its own resources, it has been forced into a position of relative helplessness in all these spheres. This accords neither with the leading role it believes Egypt has the right to play, nor with the role which many in Egypt believe it once played. Such a conviction of Egypt's rightful pre-eminence and nostalgia for a period of imagined Egyptian hegemony is widespread. The present inability of Mubarak to make a specifically Egyptian imprint on the region, commensurate with these expectations, will be ascribed either to the impersonal forces which have irrevocably altered the Middle East or to the incapacity and possibly illegitimacy of the Egyptian President himself. Whilst this is still manageable for Mubarak, his own frustration in attempting to shape a distinctive and effective role for Egypt in the region will be matched by his, and others' unease about the long term erosion of his own authority within Egypt caused by similar frustrations throughout Egyptian political society.

References

Harkabi Y (1986), *The Fateful Choices before Israel,* Text of a lecture given April 1986 at the Keck Centre for International Strategic Studies at Claremont McKenna College, distributed by the Keck Centre.

King R (1987), *The Iran-Iraq War - political implications,* Adelphi Paper 219, International Institute for Strategic Studies, London.

Kramer G (1983), L'Egypte du President Mubarak, *Politique Etrangere,* Autumn.

Shamir S (1986), Basic Dilemmas of the Mubarak Regime, *Orbis,* Vol 30 Pt 1.

Tripp C (1986), Iraq - ambitions checked, *Survival,* November/December.

Notes on the Contributors

Galal Amin is Professor of Economics at the American University in Cairo. He was visiting Professor at the University of California, Los Angeles in 1978/9 and 1985/6. His books include: *Food Supply and Economic Development* (1966), *The Modernization of Poverty* (1974), *International Migration of Egyptian Labour* (jointly with E. T. Awny, 1985), and in Arabic: *The Arab East and the West* (1983).

Nazih Ayubi is a lecturer in Politics at the University of Exeter, England. He was Visiting Associate Professor of political science at the University of California, Los Angeles from 1979 to 1983. In addition to five books in Arabic, he is the author of *Bureaucracy and Politics in Contemporary Egypt* (London: 1980). He has contributed chapters to a number of books on the Middle East, amongst the most recent of which are *The Mediterranean Region* ed. G. Luciani (London, 1984); *Beyond Coercion: The Durability of the Arab State* eds. I.W. Zartman and A. Dawisha (London: 1987).

David Butter is a graduate of Oxford University in Arabic (1978) and was awarded an MA in Comparative Politics at the University of Sussex in 1983. He worked as a news agency journalist in Beirut 1980-1982 and has been reporting for the *Middle East Economic Digest*, with Egypt as a speciality, since 1984.

Simon Commander was educated at the Universities of Oxford and Cambridge. He has worked in India and in Egypt and has recently studied the impact of structural adjustment programmes on the agricultural sector in Sub-Saharan Africa (principally Senegal, Ghana and Sierra Leone). He has also worked at the International Labour Office (Geneva), the Universities of Newcastle upon Tyne and Heidelberg. He has been a periodic consultant to various international agencies - World Bank, UNDP,

IFAD and FAO- and, until recently, was a Research Officer at the Overseas Development Instititute.

Mona Makram-Ebeid is a lecturer in Sociology at the American University in Cairo. She has lectured in several universities in the United States, writes a regular column in the *Wafd* newspaper and has had several articles published in *Al-Ahram* and *Al-Ahram Al Iqtisadi* . Her last publication was 'Mubarak: un habile funambule', in *Géopolitique Africaine*, Mai-Juin 1986. She is presently working on a book entitled *The Wafd Party:Continuity and Change*.

Roger Owen is a Fellow of St. Antony's College and a Faculty lecturer in the Recent Economic History of the Middle East at Oxford. He is also currently Director of St. Antony's College Middle East Centre. His publications include *Cotton and the Egyptian Economy 1820-1914* and *The Middle East in the World Economy 1800-1914*. He is also joint editor, with Bob Sutcliffe, of *Studies in the Theories of Imperialism*.

Hani Shukrullah is working in Cairo for a news agency whilst completing a thesis on the concept of the 'national bourgeoisie' for a Ph.D. in development sociology at Essex University. He has written extensively on the political situation in Egypt for *The Middle East* and for other publications.

Charles Tripp is a lecturer in Politics with reference to the Near and Middle East at the School of Oriental and African Studies, University of London. Until 1986, he was Assistant Director of the Programme for Strategic and International Security Studies, at the Graduate Institute of International Studies, Geneva. He is the author (with Shahram Chubin) of *Iran and Iraq at War* (1988) and editor of *Regional Security in the Middle East* (1984).

Index